Building Power in Writing

HENRY I. CHRIST

Dedicated to serving

AMSCO

our nation's youth

Amsco School Publications, Inc.
315 Hudson Street/New York, N.Y. 10013

Henry I. Christ has had a long and distinguished career as writer, editor, teacher, and supervisor. A specialist in language, literature, and composition, he has written more than a hundred textbooks in the field of English, including many published by Amsco. For nearly ten years, he was the editor of the teachers' magazine *High Points*. He has been active in professional organizations and has held office at the local, state, and national levels. A frequent speaker at English conventions and workshops throughout the United States, he has also lectured on educational television and participated in curriculum development and evaluation.

Marie E. Christ has worked with Henry I. Christ as a partner throughout his writing career. She has provided many practical suggestions and usable materials. As always, her good judgment, common sense, and hard work played a major role in the development and preparation of this book.

When ordering this book, please specify:
either **R 550 W** or BUILDING POWER IN WRITING

ISBN 0-87720-774-7

Printed in the United States of America

TO THE STUDENT

Writing has always been much
like writing a check—it is easy to write
a check if you have enough money in
the bank, and writing comes more
easily if you have something to say.

Sholem Asch

Building Power in Writing has as a major goal helping you to find something to say. You have vast untapped resources of experiences, feelings, likes, and dislikes. You are quite different from any other human being on this planet. You have opinions, too often unexpressed. You have tales to tell, too often untold. You have descriptions to share, too often filed away and forgotten.

Having something to say is most important, but being able to express this something is also important. Learning how to write easily, correctly, and forcefully is another vital goal. The ABC of good writing is simple:

A   Accuracy

B   Brevity

C   Clarity

Building Power in Writing aims to help you master these ABCs.

The book is divided into four main sections. Part I, "Review of Writing Skills," outlines the writing process and provides practice in following the important steps. It reviews the single sentence, with emphasis on the ABCs mentioned above. It discusses the organization of the paragraph, with abundant examples. Then it takes you, step by patient step, through many representative writing challenges: writing exposition, narration, description, the personal essay, the letter, the report, the summary (or précis), as well as completing common forms.

Part II is the resource section for Part I. It is an ideal reference handbook for the writing section. If you are not sure whether to say ''between you and I'' or ''between you and me,'' consult Part II. It reviews common usage errors. It starts with problems of sentence structure and then takes up all the common errors that plague you as you write. Punctuation, capitalization, and spelling round out this section.

There are two kinds of activities in Parts I and II of *Building Power in Writing*: practices and exercises. Practices have been designed for teaching as well as testing. Therefore, you will find answers to all practices at the back of the book. Suggested answers to exercises are found in a separate answer key available to teachers. For maximum help, do not look at practice answers until you have tried the practice.

Part III is a set of tests that review the material in Parts I and II. The tests may serve as a review of material covered. You may also use them as a diagnostic tool to discover your areas of weakness. Then you can turn to the appropriate chapters in the text. Handy cross-references in a number of the tests will help you find the pages you need.

Part IV is a comprehensive review of the writing skills developed in the text. They are presented in test form and may be used for additional drill in writing.

If you follow the plan suggested in this book, you will face future writing challenges with confidence.

Henry I. Christ

CONTENTS

PART I

Review of Writing Skills

PART II

Review of Common Usage Problems

PART III

Multiple-Choice Tests

PART IV

Writing Practice Tests

PART I
Review of Writing Skills

Writing is an often-misunderstood skill. When you write, you do more than put words on paper. You discover meaning in your experiences and communicate with others. Think, for a moment, of all the skills used in writing: experiencing, defining, imagining, inventing, inquiring, reasoning, organizing, discovering, problem-solving, making decisions, and, above all, learning. Because so many elements are involved, you may be overawed by the process of writing. You needn't be. When writing is broken down into smaller steps, the project becomes manageable. The sections that follow will show how writing can be a pleasurable as well as a challenging task. You know more than you realize. You have more talent than you can imagine. As a unique individual, you have something to offer in your writing that no other person can offer.

1. Steps in the Writing Process

Try Prewriting

Prewriting is the first step in the writing process. It lays the groundwork for what is to come. It makes the writing challenge less formidable. This first step includes a number of important elements to consider before you begin the first draft.

1. Explore your interests. When you go to a magazine rack, where do you tend to look? At magazines about classic cars? Quilting? Coins? Fashions? Movies? Do you like to read about football, archery, remodeling, interior decorating, television, water sports, the Olympics? Your interests are different from those of others.

Exercise 1: Choosing a Topic

Choose a general topic of interest to you. Several have just been suggested. Here are a few more to start you thinking: tropical fish, dress design, dinosaurs, detective stories, horror movies, American history, chess, surfing, comets, upholstering. Do not, however, limit yourself to these topics. Find one you are really interested in.

2. Limit the topic. "Collecting," for example, is too broad a subject. People collect objects as different as miniature ceramic owls and expensive antique cars. "Collecting Baseball Cards" is more manageable, but narrowing the topic still further might be desirable. "Baseball Card Fraud" is a limited subject that would command a lot of interest.

If you call upon a personal experience, a topic like "My Summer Vacation" would be too broad (and possibly very dull). "Our Florida Trip" is narrower and more satisfactory. Perhaps, though, the topic might be limited still further: "Our Trip to Epcot Center." As you work with the topic, you might discover that you'd like to narrow the topic still further—perhaps a description of one exhibit in detail. The ultimate selection is up to you.

Exercise 2: Limiting the Topic

Limit your topic to one that can be handled in a 150–250-word paper. If your interest is collecting stamps, try this method: set up three columns: *Too Broad*, *A Little Better*, *Better Still*. See where your topic fits. In all likelihood, your topic is too broad. Here's how a writer limited a topic on collecting stamps:

Too Broad	*A Little Better*	*Better Still*
Collecting stamps	U.S. stamps	The Columbian issue of 1893

3. Brainstorm your ideas. Brainstorming is a method of stimulating ideas about a topic you may be interested in. If, for example, you are interested in collecting baseball cards, put down everything that comes into your head about the subject, even if seemingly farfetched. Later will be time enough to exert needed control. For the moment, you want your imagination to run free.

Think for a few moments about a usable topic for brainstorming. Suppose you chose a visit to Epcot in the Disney complex near Orlando, Florida. Here are some items you might jot down during the unstressed listing of stray thoughts and subjects.

> the dinosaurs in the Universe of Energy
> strategy in visiting the exhibits: avoiding the crowds
> the separation into two main parts: Future World and World
>   Showcase
> the buses that regularly travel around the World Showcase
> the long lines early in the day
> the Land and the ride through tomorrow's agriculture
> the cleanliness

Spaceship Earth
the meaning of the word *Epcot*
the good food in the Land building
the magnificent film on China
guided tours
the Living Seas
the Monorail station
the Journey into Imagination in the Kodak building
excellent photo opportunities
location of Epcot
the World of Motion
the appropriate architecture
the inspiring American Adventure
the street show outside the Italian building
the boat ride in the Mexico building
the beautiful lagoon
convenient restaurants and rest areas
the launches that cross the lagoon

There are various kinds of writing, with different challenges. Brainstorming a research report, for example, is more demanding than brainstorming a personal-experience composition. For the former, you will call upon many different skills: reading, listening, speaking, interviewing, classifying, visualizing. On a research report, you may also work with one or more partners and brainstorm ideas together. The present introductory review of the writing process, however, will confine itself to a personal-experience composition. This review explores the basis of the writing process. You will have an opportunity later to try other writing challenges.

To increase your writing potential, you may wish to carry a writer's notebook to jot down any usable thoughts that may come to you at odd times of the day. Such a notebook can enrich your brainstorming. It can do more. Recording brief experiences, ideas, snatches of conversation, bits of observation can provide ideas and materials for the writing to come.

4. Try freewriting. This is similar to brainstorming, but instead of just listing topics, you start writing furiously. You write whatever comes to you on the topic without worrying about anything: organization, coherence, unity, or correctness. Only *you* will see this writing. It precedes the writing of the first draft.

Exercise 3: Brainstorming

Brainstorm everything that you can think about the topic you have chosen. If you prefer, try freewriting, letting ideas come to you freely without restraint.

5. Organize your ideas. Organization is necessary to create a coherent composition. The sample list on pages 2–3 shows the possibilities, but it is a hodge-podge. Group similar items together, with appropriate headings. As you organize, you will find some items that don't fit. Discard them. Add any new items that come to you as you create your outline.

Here is a possible rearrangement of the Epcot topic. Three main headings have been chosen.

Getting Around in Epcot
 the launch across the lagoon
 the buses
 the Monorail station
The Plan of Epcot
 World Showcase, with its buildings of various nations
 Future World, with its buildings dealing with technology
 convenient restaurants and rest areas
My Favorite Rides and Exhibits
 the dinosaurs in the Universe of Energy
 the Land and the ride through tomorrow's agriculture
 Spaceship Earth
 the World of Motion
 the Living Seas
 the Journey into Imagination
 the magnificent film on China
 the boatride in the Mexican building
 the street show outside the Italian building
 the inspiring American Adventure

Note that not all the brainstormed items appear in this informal outline. Some of them don't seem to fit into the composition as it is developing. In the outline, the third large group is really two: the rides and exhibits in (1) Future World and those in (2) World Showcase.

As you look at your more organized materials, you must make a decision. Do you still have too much for a modest composition? Perhaps limiting the composition still further, to Future World, would be wise.

If you decide to limit your composition just to Future World, you might want to reorganize and reach into your memory for more details. Here is a revised outline:

The Place of Future World in the Epcot Plan
 shares Epcot with World Showcase
 presents a picture of advanced technologies
 dramatizes modern advances and some of our problems
 central to meaning: Environmental Prototype
  Community of Tomorrow
Favorite Exhibits
 the Universe of Energy
 the Land
 Spaceship Earth
 World of Motion
 Journey into Imagination
My Impressions
 entertainment
 information
 relaxation

Exercise 4: Organizing an Informal Outline

Organize into an informal outline the items you have brainstormed. Don't be afraid to discard some items on that list. Add new items as they occur to you. Use the preceding example of an outline as a guide.

Write the First Draft

This is your attempt to put your many ideas on paper in a readable form. It needn't be perfect, of course, but it should suggest the main direction of your composition. The first draft of a composition on Epcot might look like this:

EPCOT'S WORLD OF TOMORROW

Epcot means "Expermental Prototype Community of Tomorrow. The goal is to show what life might be like in the years' to come. Epcot is divided into two sections. World Showcase features exhibits from many countries around the world. Future World comes closest to the theme of the park, both are exciting. Here are found advanced technologies in energy, communication food processing, and other important areas. A trip through the exhibits of Future World gives the visitor a renewed awareness of the dangers and possibilities that will face us in the years' to come. The exhibits are many and varied, my five favorites included comfortable rides. With much to see.

Spaceship Earth is a huge sphere just inside the gates of Epcot. It features a futuristic ride through it's interior. As the riders glide smoothly into the very heart of the sphere. Another thrilling ride, Universe of Energy, takes visitors back in time to the time of the dinasores. Here there aren't no small cars, instead, large sections of people-movers transport hundreds of guests together. World of Motion traces the history of transportation. Still another ride, Journey into Imagination encourages creative daydreaming, it features a flash photograph of the visitors as they ride along. The ride in the Land building is a change of pace. It travels through various ''climate zones'' and shows how food will be grown in the world of tomorrow, when even the (dessert) will have to provide food for the hungry population of the earth. I was overwelmed by Epcot. I have attended one world's fair. Epcot was better. It is a continuing world's fair. Where the frontiers of technology are displayed in an entertaining fashion. It was not as crowded as the neighboring Magic kingdom, and our family is more relaxed. We had done good to plan the visit. We were entertained and informed at the same time.

Exercise 5: Writing the First Draft

Write the first draft of your composition. Use your informal outline as a guide, but not as a straitjacket. Sometimes additional ideas come in the writing itself. Don't hesitate to incorporate good new ideas into your draft. At this stage, don't worry too much about possible errors. If you can't spell a word, just circle it, as in the sample composition. For now, just keep on writing. Get those sentences down.

Revise the First Draft

When you look at your draft with a more critical eye, you will find errors that need correcting. Exchange papers with a classmate. The classmate will undoubtedly find errors you missed; you will undoubtedly find errors for him or her. This step provides an opportunity to improve the expression as well as to correct any errors.

Pages 7 and 8 show what a revised draft might look like. Note the changes to improve the manuscript. At the end of the revised draft are explanations for the corrections made.

EPCOT'S WORLD OF TOMORROW

1   *Epcot* means "Experimental Prototype Community

2   of Tomorrow. The goal is to show what life might be

3   like in the years to come. Epcot is divided into two

4   sections. World Showcase features exhibits from many

5   countries around the world. Future World comes closest

6   to the theme of the park, both are exciting. Here are

7   found advanced technologies in energy, communication,

8   food processing, and other important areas. A trip

9   through the exhibits of Future World gives the visitor

10   a renewed awareness of the dangers and possibilities that

11   will face us in the years' to come. The exhibits are many

12   and varied, my five favorites included comfortable rides

13   With much to see.

14   Spaceship Earth is a huge sphere just inside the

15   gates of Epcot. It features a futuristic ride through it's

16   interior, As the riders glide smoothly into the very heart

17   of the sphere. Another thrilling ride, Universe of

18   Energy, takes visitors back in time to the time of the

19   dinasores. Here there aren't no small cars, instead, large

20   sections of people-movers transport hundreds of guests

21   together. World of Motion traces the history of trans-

22   portation. Still another ride, Journey into Imagination,

23   encourages creative daydreaming, It features a flash

24   photograph of the visitors as they ride along. The ride

25   in the Land building is a change of pace. It travels

26   through various "climate zones" and shows how food

27   will be grown in the world of tomorrow, when even the

28   dessert will have to provide food for the hungry popula-

29   tion of the earth. I was overwelmed by Epcot. I have

30 attended one world's fair. Epcot was better. It is a

31 continuing world's fair, Where the frontiers of

32 technology are displayed in an entertaining fashion. It

33 was not as crowded as the neighboring Magic Kingdom,

34 and our family *was* more relaxed. We had done ~~good~~ *well* to

35 plan the visit. We were entertained and informed at the

36 same time.

Reasons for the revisions are listed below. Refer to the pages in parentheses for more help with each kind of revision.

Line

1   Check the spelling of doubtful words (pages 191–201).

2   Quotation marks should be used in pairs (page 179).

3   *Years* is a plural, not a possessive (pages 143–148).

6   Avoid run-on sentences (pages 138–142).

7   Use a comma to separate items in a series (page 173).

11   *Years to come* repeats an expression in line 3.

11   Begin a new paragraph for a new idea (page 38).

12   Avoid run-on sentences (pages 138–142).

13   Avoid sentence fragments (pages 128–138).

14   The first sentence is merely an expansion of the topic sentence in lines 11–13. It should not begin a new paragraph (page 38).

15   The possessives of personal pronouns do not have apostrophes (pages 169–171).

16   Avoid sentence fragments (pages 128–138).

18   *Time* is repeated; *era* provides variety (page 17).

19   Check the spelling of doubtful words (pages 191–201).

19   Avoid the double negative (page 162).

19   Avoid run-on sentences (pages 138–142).

22   Interrupting commas should be used in pairs (page 173).

23   Avoid run-on sentences (pages 138–142).

28   Check the spelling of doubtful words (pages 191–201).

29   Begin a new paragraph for a new idea (page 38).

31   Avoid sentence fragments (pages 128–138).

33   Capitalize proper nouns (pages 185–190).

34   Keep to the same tense (pages 149–151).

34   Don't confuse adjectives and adverbs (page 161).

Exercise 6: Revising the First Draft

Using the preceding example as a guide, revise your first draft. To improve the editing, exchange papers with a classmate. You will both benefit by constructive criticism. If possible, read your paper aloud to a sympathetic listener to check its clarity and interest level.

Write the Final Draft

This is the logical next step. You have revised the original draft and are ready. You have edited and polished it. This is what a completed composition looks like.

EPCOT'S WORLD OF TOMORROW
by
Your Name

Epcot means ''Experimental Prototype Community of Tomorrow.'' The goal is to show what life might be like in the years to come. Epcot is divided into two sections. World Showcase features exhibits from many countries around the world. Future World comes closest to the theme of the park, but both are exciting. Here are found advanced technologies in energy, communication, food processing, and many other important areas. A trip through the exhibits of Future World gives the visitor a renewed awareness of the dangers and possibilities that will face us in the 21st century.

The exhibits are many and varied. My five favorites included comfortable rides with much to see. Spaceship Earth is a huge sphere just inside the gates of Epcot. It features a futuristic ride through its interior as the riders glide smoothly into the very heart of the sphere. Another thrilling ride, Universe of Energy, takes visitors back in time to the era of the dinosaurs. Here there aren't any small cars. Instead, large sections of people-movers transport hundreds of guests together. World of Motion traces the history of transportation. Still another ride, Journey into Imagination, encourages creative daydreaming. It features a flash photograph of the visitors as they ride along. The ride in the Land building is a change of pace. It travels through various ''climate zones'' and shows how food will be grown in the world of tomorrow, when even the desert will have to provide food for the hungry population of the earth.

I was overwhelmed by Epcot. I have attended one world's fair. Epcot was better. It is a continuing world's fair where the frontiers of technology are displayed in an entertaining fashion. It was not as crowded as the neighboring Magic Kingdom, and our family was more relaxed. We had done well to plan the visit. We were entertained and informed at the same time.

Exercise 7: Writing the Final Copy

After you have revised your first draft, write the final copy of your composition. Then read it one more time to make sure it represents your best thinking on your topic. *Proofread* the final copy for any remaining errors by carefully checking it against your revised first draft. Finally, your name should appear below the title as the author of your composition.

Find Your Audience

This is the last step in the writing process. You will want others to read your paper. Classmates, friends, or relatives may be interested in what you have written. If you have truly expressed your individual needs and likes, your teacher will look forward to reading your composition.

Exercise 8: Publishing Your Article

Writing involves communication between individuals. ''Publish'' your article by choosing a reader or listener. Perhaps the individual student papers can be gathered into a class booklet.

Looking Ahead

Now that you have had a general review of the writing process, you are ready for a more specific review of types of writing. You will start with a review of the single sentence, proceed to the paragraph, and then practice various types of writing:

persuasion	business letter
explanation	friendly letter
narration	report
description	summary
personal essay	forms

2. Writing the Single Sentence

In the famous French play *The Bourgeois Gentleman,* the major character is a tradesman who hopes to rise in society and become a gentleman. He tries to ape the manners of those above him in the social scale. At one point, though, Monsieur Jourdain is delighted to learn that he has a skill equal to that of the gentry. He says, "Good Heavens! For more than forty years I have been speaking prose without knowing it."

You are like Monsieur Jourdain. For most of your life, you have been speaking and writing prose. You are far more competent than you realize. As a native speaker of English, you understand the structure of the language. You easily handle such major problems as word order. Though the etiquette of language is sometimes a minor stumbling block (pages 122–201), you know more English structure than an intelligent adult who is learning English as a second language. You can build on your native skill in language.

All writing begins with the sentence; yet the sentence is often ignored, left to watch out for itself. This section will direct your attention to the sentence. It will ask you to judge between good and bad sentences. It will encourage you to write some good sentences. The French writer Anatole France once wrote, "Caress your sentence tenderly; it will end up smiling at you."

Characteristics of Good Sentences

Sentences are of many types, varied in style and subject matter. Yet good sentences have certain qualities in common.

1. Good sentences don't waste words. They use only enough words to carry the thought. They don't wander. They make their point . . . and stop (pages 17–20).

   Wordy: The difficulties we cause in this all-too-brief life of ours are often those that we bring upon ourselves, even if unintentionally.

   Economical: Most of the shadows of this life are caused by our standing in our own sunshine. (Ralph Waldo Emerson)

2. Good sentences are clear. They express a thought clearly and directly (pages 20–25).

   Muddled: Gil got up to bat and sent it into the right-field stands.

   Clear: Gil got up to bat and sent the ball into the right-field stands.

3. Good sentences have unity. They stick to one general topic in a sentence (pages 34–37).

   Lacking in unity: Good tennis players don't have to work very hard, but golfers sometimes seem to enjoy the game more.

   Unified: If you see a tennis player who looks as if he is working very hard, then that means he isn't very good. (Helen Wills Moody)

4. Good sentences are coherent, using accurate connectives (pages 21–22).

   Lacking coherence: Because Sue was our best pitcher, she didn't get a chance to pitch in the playoffs.

   Coherent: Although Sue was our best pitcher, she didn't get a chance to pitch in the playoffs.

5. Good sentences are varied in structure. They do not always follow a set pattern (pages 25–34).

   Monotonous: Edgar is handsome and rich. He is also a fine artist. I envy him.

   Varied: Edgar is not only handsome and rich, but also a fine artist. How I envy him!

6. Good sentences call upon strong, specific nouns and vivid verbs to carry the thought. They use adjectives and adverbs sparingly but effectively (pages 18–19).

   Dull: The duck landed on the ice unsuccessfully and finally came to a stop after a long slide along the ice on the pond.

   Vivid: The mallard landed uncertainly on the ice, skidded and flopped along for twenty feet, and then scrambled to its feet with dignity.

7. Good sentences are pleasing to read, usually an enjoyable part of a larger whole (pages 38, 122–128).

8. Good sentences are complete, neither fragments (pages 128–138) nor run-ons (pages 138–142).

9. Good sentences are technically correct, using correct usage (pages 122–190) and correct spelling (pages 191–201).

Comparing Sentences

A helpful activity is to read good sentences written by others. An example of a splendid, simple sentence is this by Martin Luther King, Jr.

"At the center of nonviolence stands the principle of love."

How much less effective it would have been if stated in this way:

> People who believe in nonviolence and practice it are really showing that they love others.

The first sentence is direct, clear, economical.

Exercise 1: Comparing Sentences

Which sentence in each pair do you consider better? Tell why.

1. *a.* We went on the roller coaster and then we went on the flume ride and then we went on the monorail.
   b. We went on the roller coaster, the flume ride, and the monorail.

   _____

   _____

2. *a.* At the library, I picked up a Sherlock Holmes detective story and a book about photography.
   b. I went to the library and I picked up a detective story about Sherlock Holmes and a book that tells all about photography.

   _____

   _____

3. *a.* The family had all agreed on a camping spot for our vacation, and Brad suddenly disagreed.
   b. The family had all agreed on a camping spot for our vacation, but Brad suddenly disagreed.

   _____

   _____

Proverbs

Proverbs contain folk wisdom. They compress a lot of meaning into a small space. Proverbs are usually good sentences to imitate. Here are ten proverbs—short but complete sentences.

> A burnt child dreads the fire.
> Actions speak louder than words.
> Soft words don't scratch the tongue.
> Always have two strings to your bow.
> Every man is his brother's keeper.
> Man shall not live by bread alone.
> Expect to be treated as you have treated others.
> Don't saw off the branch you're sitting on.
> If you want to lead, you must be able to follow.
> The bigger they are, the harder they fall.

Exercise 2: Restating Proverbs

Try your skill. Select three of the proverbs listed above. For each one write a one-sentence restatement. Try to capture the same meaning. Study the examples below.

EXAMPLES:

Original: You never miss the water till the well runs dry.
Restated: You often fail to appreciate things until you lose them.

Original: As you make your bed, so you must lie on it.
Restated: You must pay for the mistakes you make.

_____

_____

_____

_____

_____

_____

Completing Comparisons

"The baseball players gathered around the umpire like angry bees."

If you paid close attention to your speech, you would find that you use many comparisons in the course of a day. Some are **direct**, with *like* or *as*: "as strong as an ox," "as timid as a mouse," "like a lion." Others are **indirect**: "Joan was a tiger on the field." (Joan played as savagely as a tiger.) Both of them are a kind of poetry. Try your skill in writing sentences with comparisons.

Exercise 3: Completing Comparisons

Select three of the following and complete each with an original comparison. Study the example below.

EXAMPLE:

A book is like . . .

A book is like a treasure chest waiting to be opened.

1. A rainstorm is like . . .
2. A kitten is like . . .
3. A wild deer is like . . .
4. A forest fire is like . . .
5. Riding a bicycle is like . . .

6. The school cafeteria is like . . .
7. A good friend is like . . .
8. The city at night is like . . .
9. Lightning is like . . .
10. Swimming in the ocean is like . . .

_____

_____

_____

_____

_____

_____

Exercise 4: Completing Sentences

Select five of the following and complete each to make a good sound sentence.

1. My major ambition in life is to . . .
2. This evening, after dinner, I am planning . . .
3. My favorite way to spend Saturday is to . . .
4. Last summer, I . . .
5. Television . . .
6. For dessert . . .
7. When the game was over . . .
8. I hope . . .
9. At the end of the movie . . .
10. Why didn't . . .

1. own my own dance company
10. the cops get convicted in the Rodney King case
5. is society's key to the mind
4. got beat up
2. go outside and not get shot

Exercise 5: Writing Sentences

Write a good, single sentence that tells about each of the following.

EXAMPLE:

a favorite pet

I once had a parakeet named Humphrey, who enjoyed flying around the room.

1. an unusual coincidence that occurred recently

   My friend and I traded places

2. a very happy moment in your life

   When my little sister was born.

3. something you are proud of

   Being put in PSAT math

4. a surprise

   My mother is adopting a baby boy.

5. the winning point

   When I swam the last I am in a meet and won.

Exercise 6: Brainstorming Sentences

Now that you have had practice in writing various sentences, try brainstorming some of your own. Write six sentences "off the top of your head" on any subject that appeals to you.

Malcom X was a great black leader.
Marcus Garvey started the Back to Africa.
People of every color need to unite.
Unity is the key to ending prejudice.
In the future I plan to own my own dance company.
I feel racial prejudice is wrong.

Exercise 7: Revising Sentences

Reread your six brainstormed sentences and rewrite them in correct form. Save the sentences in this section. You may wish to use one or more of them in later writing assignments.

Malcom X did a lot for the black race.
Marcus Garvey was the pioneer for the Back to Africa movement.
The world as a whole needs to unite.
Unity is the key to ending prejudice.
In the future I plan to own my own dance company.
Prejudice between racial cultures is wrong

3. Writing Clear, Forceful Sentences

Good writing has four major characteristics: economy, clarity, variety, and unity.

Economy

Never make a thought more complicated than it really is. If you can express yourself simply and directly, do so. Here are some errors to avoid.

Useless Words

Eliminate all useless words.

Wordy: At the soccer match, Joel met up with two friends from elementary school.

Concise: At the soccer match, Joel met two friends from elementary school.

Duplication

Avoid saying the same thing twice, even though in different words.

Wordy: We flew by air to Cleveland and returned back by bus.

Concise: We flew to Cleveland and returned by bus.

Wordy Construction

Don't use too many words to express an idea. Condense a phrase (see page 129) to a word, a clause to a phrase or even a word. Be a *which* hunter and eliminate all unnecessary *whiches*.

Wordy: The newscast which was televised this morning on a local station described a suspicious car which had a license plate from the state of North Dakota.

Concise: This morning's local television newscast described a suspicious car with a North Dakota license plate.

Pretentious Language

Unless you are being humorous, don't use a longer word if a simpler word will do the job. Save the longer word for a context in which the simpler word is not as meaningful.

Pretentious: The feline member of our family loves to frolic, gambol, and cavort for considerable periods of time with the canine member of our family menage.

Simpler: Our cat often plays with the family dog.

Note: The first sentence might be acceptable in a humorous essay that mocks pretension.

Piled-up Modifiers

Don't pile adjective upon adjective, adverb upon adverb. Where possible, use specific nouns and verbs to reduce the number of modifiers.

Wordy: The young, immature baby of but a year walked unsteadily and shakily across the floor into the outstretched, waiting arms of her waiting mother.

Concise: The one-year-old tottered across the floor into her mother's outstretched arms.

Practice 1: Studying Conciseness

Answers to Practice 1 and all practices in *Building Power in Writing* can be found in the back of the book. Do not consult the answers till you have tried the practice.

In each pair of sentences, choose the more economical and point out why the chosen sentence is preferable.

1. *a.* The house which stood on the corner of Main Street and Maple Avenue has been declared a landmark with historic associations.
   b. The house on the corner of Main Street and Maple Avenue has been declared a historic landmark.

   _____

   _____

2. *a.* July daytime temperatures this year have averaged about 73 degrees.
   b. July temperatures during the day this year have averaged about 73 degrees on the average.

   _____

   _____

3. *a.* The Paso Fino is a relatively small horse with a distinctive, appealing gait.
   b. Of the equine breed, the Paso Fino is a horse that is relatively small but with a gait that is as distinctive as it is appealing.

   _____

   _____

4. *a.* The Chrono watch is cheap in price but efficient in use.
   b. The Chrono watch is cheap but efficient.

   _____

   _____

5. *a.* When Ted found he had lost his keys, he rushed to the store he had just left.
   b. When Ted found he had carelessly and thoughtlessly lost his keys, he rushed rapidly and swiftly into the store he had just left.

   _____

   _____

Exercise 1: Writing Concisely

Rewrite the following selections to make them more concise. Keep in mind the preceding suggestions.

1. The bus that I take to school seems to have one shock absorber that is faulty.

   _____

   _____

2. My favorite pet among all pets is the canine pet.

   _____

   _____

3. My brother owns a beautiful cat that has long hair.

   _____

   _____

4. In *Tom Sawyer* it tells the story of a boy on the Mississippi.

   _____

   _____

5. The Biltmore House in Asheville is a magnificent house, probably the largest mansion in the nation.

   _____

   _____

Exercise 2: Identifying Familiar Proverbs

Identify the familiar proverb in each of the following sentences.

1. The bird that is on the job early is the one that catches his morning meal, the worm.

   _____

   _____

2. A child who has, unfortunately, been burnt is certain to dread the fire, for fear of repetition.

   _____

   _____

3. Always look in all directions before you propel yourself into the unknown.

   _____

   _____

4. Having an overabundance of cooks is likely to have a negative effect on the broth being prepared.

   _____

   _____

5. The grassy vegetation seems a more attractive shade of green when noticed on the other side of the fence.

   _____

   _____

Clarity

Write clearly as well as concisely. Here are some errors to avoid.

Unclear Antecedents

Make certain that a pronoun has a clear antecedent (pages 166–167). Reword the sentences or supply a needed noun.

Confusing: Use that towel to mop your brow and put it in the clothes hamper. (The brow or the towel?)

Clear: Use that towel to mop your brow and put the towel in the clothes hamper.

Confusing: If papers are left behind by untidy hikers, burn them.

Clear: Any papers left behind by untidy hikers should be burned.

Quote the speaker's actual words if necessary to make the meaning clearer.

Confusing: Sally told her mother that she had left the lawn sprinklers on.
(Is the antecedent of "she" Sally or her mother?)

Clear: Sally told her mother, "I left the lawn sprinklers on."

Clear: Sally told her mother, "You left the lawn sprinklers on."

Dangling Modifiers

A modifier dangles if it is placed so that it seems to modify a word it was not intended to modify. Put a modifier close to the word it modifies. Sometimes the word itself must be supplied.

Dangling: Turning the corner, the post office was on the left.
(The post office was not turning the corner.)

Clear: Turning the corner, I noticed the post office on my left.

Clear: As I turned the corner, I noticed the post office on my left.

Confusing: Terry saw a deer riding her bike through the Hopkins meadow.

Clear: Riding her bike through the Hopkins meadow, Terry saw a deer.

Confusing: At the age of three, Mark's mother remarried.

Clear: When Mark was three, his mother remarried.

Confusing: While working in the library, a new shipment of books arrived.

Clear: While I was working in the library, a new shipment of books arrived.

Confusing: At the party, packages were given to all the children filled with Halloween candy.
(The children may be filled later!)

Clear: At the party, packages filled with Halloween candy were given to all the children.

Inaccurate Connectives

Use the connective that expresses your thought accurately.

Confusing: I wanted to go skating, and Marcia preferred hiking.

Clear: I wanted to go skating, but Marcia preferred hiking.

Confusing: Because Nancy was on a visit to her ill grandmother, she still got her term paper in on time.

Clear: Although Nancy was on a visit to her ill grandmother, she still got her term paper in on time.

The Inexact Word

Be sure to choose the word you need to express your thought accurately.

Confusing: Our Saturday project is to install all broken windows in the school.

Clear: Our Saturday project is to replace all broken windows in the school.

Confusing: Don't fail to miss tonight's rerun of *Star Trek*.

Clear: Don't miss tonight's rerun of *Star Trek*.

Clear: Don't fail to see tonight's rerun of *Star Trek*.

Practice 2: Choosing Clear Sentences

In each pair of sentences, choose the clearer one and point out why the chosen sentence is preferable.

1. *a.* Listening for a cardinal's song, my attention was captured by the cawing of a crow.
   b. As I was listening for a cardinal's song, my attention was captured by the cawing of a crow.

   _____

   _____

2. *a.* Maria told Consuelo, ''You've just won the athlete-of-the month award.''
   b. Maria told Consuelo that she had just won the athlete-of-the-month award.

   _____

   _____

3. *a.* We thought everyone had accepted Hank's suggestion, and suddenly Jason got up to object strongly.
   b. We thought everyone had accepted Hank's suggestion, but suddenly Jason got up to object strongly.

   _____

   _____

4. *a.* Regular attendance is a major cause of failure in school.
   b. Irregular attendance is a major cause of failure in school.

   _____

   _____

5. *a.* I used moist heat for my sore elbow, and it disappeared.
   b. I used moist heat for my sore elbow, and the soreness disappeared.

   _____

   _____

Exercise 3: Writing Clearly

Rewrite the following selections to make them clearer. Keep in mind the preceding suggestions.

1. Grandma loves to watch passersby sitting in her chair on the porch.

   _____

   _____

2. Carl told his brother that he had been accepted at Duke University.

   _____

   _____

3. Because Ellen had been away for the summer vacation, she still was able to return for Sandra's birthday party.

   _____

   _____

4. Having misplaced my ticket, my chance of seeing the Bulls play the Lakers was slim.

   _____

   _____

5. The problem of driving to Craggy Gardens on the Blue Ridge Parkway was good visibility.

   _____

   _____

Vague, General Words

To add clarity and forcefulness to your writing, use specific words.

Vague: We walked up a steep peak and rejoiced at the top.

Specific: We clambered up the cone of Mt. Katahdin and shouted, ''We made it!''

Vague: On our western trip, we visited three national parks.

Specific: On our western trip, we visited Rocky Mountain National Park, Grand Canyon, and Bryce Canyon.

Vague: We had several different kinds of transportation.

Specific: We tried horseback riding, canoeing, and helicoptering.

Exercise 4: Identifying Concrete Words

In each member of the following pair, write the word or phrase that is more specific, more concrete.

1. golden retriever, dog   1. _____
2. horse, thoroughbred   2. _____
3. sport, soccer   3. _____
4. daisy, flower   4. _____
5. reptile, rattlesnake   5. _____
6. tangerine, fruit   6. _____
7. penny, coin   7. _____
8. animal, cheetah   8. _____
9. Mars, planet   9. _____
10. color, ultramarine   10. _____

Exercise 5: Using Specific Words

From the list below, select a more specific word or phrase for each italicized word or phrase in the sentences.

basketball players	*Gone with the Wind*	*Newsweek*
City Hall	hectic	purple
English	jittery	soared
flounder	lemon meringue pie	strode
football game	peas	sycamore
gazed	plunged	Thanksgiving
glider	poured	waddled
grandmother	*Macbeth*	woodworking

1. During *a holiday*, we visited my *relative* in Seattle and went to a *game*.

   _____

   _____

2. For our main meal, we had *a vegetable*, *a fish*, and a delicious *dessert*.

   _____

   _____

3. In *school*, we studied *a play*.

   _____

   _____

4. The duck *walked* along the edge of the pond and then *went* into the water.

_____

_____

5. I've always admired that sturdy *tree* that stands near *a building*.

_____

_____

6. In the *plane*, we *flew* above the fields below. Mark was *upset*.

_____

_____

7. The *athletes came* out of the plane and *went* to a waiting bus.

_____

_____

8. As we *looked* at the sunset, we noticed that *a color* predominated.

_____

_____

9. I enjoy *a hobby* especially when I am tired, after a *hard* day.

_____

_____

10. I visited the library and took out *a book* and *a magazine*.

_____

_____

Variety

To keep your readers interested, introduce variety into your writing. Don't get into a rut. For maximum effect, vary both the length and type of sentence.

Length of Sentence

Conciseness is always a desirable goal. By avoiding padding and unnecessary words, you can create a concise sentence. Note that the following sentences use words economically, though they vary in length.

Short: In fair weather, prepare for foul.   (Thomas Fuller)

Longer: If you think you're tops, you won't do much climbing.
(Arnold Glasow)

Still longer: There is only one thing better than making a new friend and that is keeping an old one.   (Elmer G. Leterman)

Type of Sentence

For variety, use an occasional question, exclamation, or command, but don't overdo.

Question: Where did I leave my tennis racket?

Exclamation: I just remembered—the public courts!

Command: Call the pro shop and say I'm on my way.

Polite request: Please let my mother know I'll be late.

Subject-Not-First Sentence

Avoid monotony. Don't begin every sentence with the subject. When a shift in placement is both natural and effective, begin a sentence with a word other than the subject. Again, don't overdo.

Adverb: Wearily, the home team went onto the field for the fifteenth inning.

Adverb phrase: After much soul-searching, Carla decided to enroll in a pre-med course.

Adverb clause: Although yellow sweet corn is more abundant in our area, Dad and I prefer the white.

There: There are still many undiscovered galaxies.

Prepositional phrase: Contrary to popular belief, a person's hair cannot turn white overnight.

Participial phrase: Finding the passage blocked, the cave explorers retraced their steps.

Infinitive phrase: To melt its way through spring snows, the skunk cabbage runs temperatures higher than its surroundings.

Prepositional phrase with gerund: Before starting the car, adjust seat belts and rearview mirrors.

Appositive: A language expert for the United Nations, Georges Schmidt can translate 66 languages.

Practice 3: Studying Subject-Not-First Sentences

In each of the following, point out the element that has been placed before the subject for variety.

1. Long after his death, Herman Melville became famous as a great American writer.

_____

_____

2. Energetically, the children at the birthday party swung at the piñata, hoping to release the candy inside.

   _____

   _____

3. Although fish are natural inhabitants of the sea, they can become seasick.

   _____

   _____

4. Checking the planet for life forms, Dr. Spock peered at his instruments.

   _____

   _____

5. A newcomer to politics, Dwight D. Eisenhower had to learn to compromise.

   _____

   _____

Exercise 6: Practicing Subject-Not-First Sentences

   Revise each of the sentences by placing a word or words before the subject.

1. The liquid inside young coconuts can be substituted for blood plasma in an emergency.

   _____

   _____

2. Only seven poems by Emily Dickinson were published during her lifetime.

   _____

   _____

3. Florence Nightingale spent the last 50 years of her life as an invalid because she had been weakened by a fever during the Crimean War.

   _____

   _____

4. Monica Seles triumphantly raised her arms in the air after defeating Steffi Graf. (two possibilities)

   _____

   _____

5. Bobby Fischer, who was a chess genius, went on to win the world championship in 1972. (two possibilities)

   _____

   _____

Appositives

Use appositives to achieve conciseness and vary the sentence structure.

Without appositives: The eagle, which is the U.S. national symbol, won out over the turkey, which was Benjamin Franklin's choice.

With appositives: The eagle, the U.S. national symbol, won out over the turkey, Benjamin Franklin's choice.

Without appositives: A thick slice of bread that was stale and unappetizing was once used as the dinner plate.

With appositives: A thick slice of bread, stale and unappetizing, was once used as the dinner plate.

Practice 4: Identifying Appositives

Point out the appositives in each of the following and tell what noun each is associated with.

1. Byron White, an All-American football player at the University of Colorado, became a Justice of the Supreme Court.

   _____

2. Copper Canyon, a huge cleft in the earth of northwestern Mexico, is the home of the Tarahumara Indians.

   _____

3. Sea otters, the playboys of the seas, are fascinating to watch.

   _____

4. Caligula, ruthless emperor of Rome, got his name from the military boots he wore as a child.

   _____

5. George Washington Carver, pioneering plant experimenter, developed 49 separate dyes from the scuppernong grape.

   _____

Exercise 7: Using Appositives

In each of the following, substitute an appositive for a clause or a sentence.

1. Napoleon Bonaparte, who was a military genius, had once been expelled from the army in disgrace.

   _____

   _____

2. Connemara is a lovely old estate in Flat Rock, North Carolina. It was once the home of the poet Carl Sandburg.

_____

_____

3. The cornea, which is an important part of the eye's structure, takes its oxygen directly from the air.

_____

_____

4. Ted Moorhead, who is always happy and upbeat, is a source of inspiration to his friends.

_____

_____

5. Chester Carlson was the inventor of the dry copying process. He had previously had the idea for the ballpoint pen.

_____

_____

Compound Subjects

Where possible, combine two separate sentences into a single sentence with a compound subject.

Two sentences: Fran supported the new cafeteria regulations. The twins also supported them.

Compound subject: Fran and the twins supported the new cafeteria regulations.

Compound Predicates

Avoid the *and I, and we, and they* habit. Use an occasional compound predicate instead of a compound sentence or two separate sentences.

Compound sentence: I visited the local library and there I found the latest mystery by P. D. James.

Compound predicate: I visited the local library and there found the latest mystery by P. D. James.

Two sentences: *Gone with the Wind* was rejected many times. It was finally published.

Compound predicate: *Gone with the Wind* was rejected many times but was finally published.

Practice 5: Studying Compound Subjects and Compound Predicates

In each of the following pairs of sentences, point out which one contains a compound subject or a compound predicate. Write the letter of your answer on the line at the left.

_____ 1. *a.* Ginnie loves Chinese egg rolls. Tammy does too.
       b. Ginnie and Tammy love Chinese egg rolls.

_____ 2. *a.* Esther enrolled in a quilting course and expects to travel to Knoxville in July.
      b. Esther enrolled in a quilting course, and she expects to travel to Knoxville in July.

_____ 3. *a.* The Peace Corps helps Third World nations with their problems. It also broadens the lives of the volunteers.
      b. The Peace Corps helps Third World nations with their problems and also broadens the lives of the volunteers.

_____ 4. *a.* Presidents Ronald Reagan and George Bush sought closer ties with the Soviet Union.
      b. President Ronald Reagan sought closer ties with the Soviet Union. President Bush did also.

_____ 5. *a.* Charles Babbage thought out the basic pinciples of modern computers. He didn't have electronic solutions for his challenges.
      b. Charles Babbage thought out the basic principles of modern computers but didn't have electronic solutions for his challenges.

Exercise 8: Using Compound Subjects and Compound Predicates

Condense each of the following by substituting compound subjects and compound predicates for pairs of simple sentences or for compound sentences.

1. Sis went to the Florida-Clemson game. Darlene also went.

_____

_____

2. Bud completed the bookcase. Then he began the chest of drawers.

_____

_____

3. We visited Grand Canyon and then we headed toward the Petrified Forest.

_____

_____

4. Nan's uncle appeared on *Jeopardy*, and he was the champion for three days.

_____

_____

5. In the Midwest, Notre Dame usually has a strong football team. So does Michigan.

_____

_____

Complex Sentences

Avoid a string of simple or compound sentences. Use complex sentences (page 125) to add variety and show more accurately the connection between ideas. By using complex sentences, you can avoid overusing *and*, *but*, and *so*.

Simple sentences: Thomas Edison was still in possession of his sight. He found braille preferable to visual reading.

Complex sentence: Though he was still in possession of his sight, Thomas Edison found braille preferable to visual reading.

Compound sentence: The thin atmosphere at 12,000 feet above sea level barely supports fire, and La Paz, Bolivia, is nearly a fireproof city.

Complex sentence: Because the thin atmosphere at 12,000 feet above sea level barely supports fire, La Paz, Bolivia, is nearly a fireproof city.

Practice 6: Studying Complex Sentences

Point out the complex sentence in each of the following pairs by writing the letter of the correct choice and then writing the subordinate clause.

1. *a.* We must support efforts to save wild plants. They may yet provide cures for presently incurable diseases.
   b. Because wild plants may yet provide cures for presently incurable diseases, we must support efforts to save them.

_____

_____

2. *a.* When Harvey arrived late at the meeting, we all greeted him in stony silence.
   b. Harvey arrived late at the meeting. We all greeted him in stony silence.

_____

_____

3. *a.* Because the Navajo language is difficult to master, it was used as a code by the United States in World War II.
   b. The Navajo language is difficult to master, and it was used as a code by the United States in World War II.

   _____

   _____

4. *a.* Berengaria, wife of Richard the Lion-Hearted, was queen of England. She never even visited there.
   b. Although Berengaria, wife of Richard the Lion-Hearted, was queen of England, she never even visited there.

   _____

   _____

5. *a.* While Charlotte was weeding the vegetable patch, Dan was watering the extensive lawn.
   b. Charlotte was weeding the vegetable patch, and Dan was watering the extensive lawn.

   _____

   _____

Exercise 9: Creating Complex Sentences

By using proper connectives (page 21), combine each of the following into a sound complex sentence.

1. Terry loses. He is always a good sport.

   _____

   _____

2. Some major artists struggled in poverty during their lifetimes. Pablo Picasso was famous and wealthy.

   _____

   _____

3. I took twelve golf lessons. Then I felt more confident on the course. (*Hint:* Use *after.*)

   _____

   _____

4. The bison population in North America was hunted mercilessly. The numbers dropped from perhaps 13 million to a few hundred.

   _____

   _____

5. Harry S Truman had been expected to lose the election. He won a smashing victory over Thomas E. Dewey.

_____

_____

Using Verbals

For variety, introduce verbals (pages 134–138) into your writing.

Without participle: I discovered an interest in various kinds of mushrooms. I decided to take a course in botany.

With participle: Having discovered an interest in various kinds of mushrooms, I decided to take a course in botany.

Without gerund: We all celebrated with milkshakes after we had won the softball championship.

With gerund: We all celebrated with milkshakes after winning the softball championship.

Without infinitive: Lars read *Plutarch's Lives* in order that he might learn more about the Roman emperors.

With infinitive: Lars read *Plutarch's Lives* to learn more about the Roman emperors.

Practice 7: Identifying Verbals

In each of the following pairs of sentences, point out the verbal by writing the letter of the correct choice and then writing the verbal.

1. *a.* After gathering the suspects together, the detective Hercule Poirot identified the murderer.
   b. The detective Hercule Poirot gathered the suspects together and identified the murderer.

_____

2. *a.* So that she might be sure of a seat for the rock concert, Shelley got on line early in the morning.
   b. To be sure of a seat for the rock concert, Shelly got on line early in the morning.

_____

3. *a.* Having studied Spanish for three years in high school, Paul nervously asked directions in Bogotá.
   b. After he had studied Spanish for three years in high school, Paul nervously asked directions in Bogotá.

_____

4. *a.* Before you leave the house, close all the windows.
   b. Before leaving the house, close all the windows.

   _____

5. *a.* In order that he might get a part in the school play, Doug read the play over and over.
   b. To get a part in the school play, Doug read the play over and over.

   _____

Exercise 10: Using Verbals

Improve these sentences by using verbals for some of the verbs.

1. Before he found the perfect filament for a light bulb, Thomas Edison unsuccessfully tried hundreds.

   _____

   _____

2. Max saved his money for years in order that he might buy a Thunderbird convertible.

   _____

   _____

3. Juan heard the score of the Rams-Lions game. He told us all at dinner.

   _____

   _____

4. Sue haunted flea markets in order that she might add to her collection of old records.

   _____

   _____

5. Spiders help humans. They destroy a hundred times their number in insects. (*Hint:* use *by.*)

   _____

   _____

Unity

Be sure that every part of a sentence is related to one main idea.

Lack of Unity

Correct a lack of unity by breaking a sentence into shorter sentences or by subordinating one part of a sentence to a main part. (Review pages 31–33, 125, 139–142.)

Lacking unity: The cockroach is a survivor, and the body can survive for weeks if the head is carefully removed.

Having unity: The cockroach is a survivor. The body can survive for weeks if the head is carefully removed.

Lacking unity: The ancestors of the horse were only a foot tall, and modern Percherons may stand over five feet at the shoulders.

Having unity: Although the ancestors of the horse were only a foot tall, modern Percherons may stand over five feet at the shoulders.

Overlapping Construction

Avoid a series of *that*, *which*, or *who* clauses. Too many make a sentence unwieldy.

Unwieldy: In the 1860s, a New York firm offered a prize which would be awarded for a satisfactory substitute for ivory which was used in the manufacture of billiard balls which were in demand because of the growing popularity of billiards.

Manageable: In the 1860s, a New York firm offered a prize for an ivory substitute. Ivory had been used in the manufacture of billiard balls for the increasingly popular game of billiards.

Parallel Structure

Be sure items are parallel. Ordinarily, *and* and *but* connect like grammatical elements—for example, two or more nouns, verbs, adjectives, phrases, or clauses.

Not parallel: At camp, we most enjoyed swimming, hiking, and how to play volleyball.

Parallel: At camp, we most enjoyed swimming, hiking, and playing volleyball.

Not parallel: Our dog Jolly is tiny, a rich brown coat, and a perky disposition.

Parallel: Our dog Jolly is tiny, wears a rich brown coat, and has a perky disposition.

Not parallel: The atmosphere of the earth filters the sun's rays, and making the sun seem unusually red at sunset.

Parallel: The atmosphere of the earth filters the sun's rays and makes the sun seem unusually red at sunset.

Practice 8: Studying Unified Structure

In each pair of sentences, point out the unified sentence or sentences. Tell why your choice is preferable.

1. *a.* I checked the bus schedule for the time of departure from Orlando and when the bus arrives at Tampa.
   b. I checked the bus schedule for the time of departure from Orlando and arrival at Tampa.

   _____

   _____

2. *a.* The path to the summit of Mt. Katahdin is rough, steep, and challenging.
   b. The path to the summit of Mt. Katahdin is rough, steep, and it is challenging.

   _____

   _____

3. *a.* Throughout the world, the number of languages is decreasing rapidly. Once there were more than a thousand languages in the New World alone.
   b. Throughout the world, the number of languages is decreasing rapidly, and once there were more than a thousand languages in the New World alone.

   _____

   _____

4. *a.* To run the domestic affairs of the White House, President Andrew Johnson depended on his daughter who bought two Jersey cows which provided fresh milk and butter which was used for the White House table.
   b. To run the domestic affairs of the White House, President Andrew Johnson depended on his daughter. She bought two Jersey cows to provide fresh milk and butter for the White House table.

   _____

   _____

5. *a.* The ideal dog is loyal, friendly, and is in good health.
   b. The ideal dog is loyal, friendly, and healthy.

   _____

   _____

Exercise 11: Improving Sentence Unity

Make each of the following unified. Follow the suggestions in the preceding pages.

1. The well-rounded tennis player has a good serve, a strong forehand, and he must have a dependable backhand.

_____

_____

2. John F. Kennedy was the first U.S. President to be born in the twentieth century, and he didn't take office until 1961.

_____

_____

3. James Madison was the shortest President, who was only five feet four inches tall and who weighed only a hundred pounds.

_____

_____

4. A professional basketball player should be tall, agile, with a great deal of courage.

_____

_____

5. Four times the Wright brothers flew that first airbound plane which was finally struck by a gust of wind which overturned it and wrecked it.

_____

_____

4. Writing the Paragraph

You have been writing single sentences that are complete in themselves. The next step in the art of writing is the paragraph. The ideal paragraph, like each of the single sentences in the preceding two sections, develops one idea.

Paragraphs vary greatly in length, but each one says, in effect, ''Here is something new.'' The first line of a new paragraph is indented to indicate that ''something new'' is coming.

As a general rule, when you write, begin a new paragraph:

in a *description*—when you change the mood or the point of view

in an *explanation*—when you begin to develop a new idea

in a *story*—when you change the time, the place, or the action

in a *written conversation*—when you change the speaker

The paragraph of explanation, often called the **expository paragraph**, is a good paragraph to work with. It calls for all the skills you'll need in writing any paragraph. Paragraphs of this type have certain characteristics.

Characteristics of Good Expository Paragraphs

1. A good paragraph develops one topic and sticks to that topic. It often provides a *topic sentence* to help the reader know what's ahead.
2. A good paragraph supports the topic sentence with examples, details, comparisons.
3. A good paragraph is arranged in a sensible, easy-to-follow order. It uses connecting words like *this*, *since*, *when*, *and*, *but*, *which* to tie parts of the paragraph together.
4. A good paragraph has interest-catching beginnings and forceful endings.
5. A good paragraph uses vivid, exact words.

Study the following paragraph to see how these characteristics apply.

The earth has a diameter of nearly 8,000 miles, but life on earth outside the sea depends upon a thin layer of topsoil. This priceless resource, rarely more than a foot or two deep, supports all the world's agriculture. Every farmer in every land depends upon the fertility of this fragile skin. All the cattle and other domesticated animals depend upon it for grazing. All the trees and shrubs need it for their food. Through the vegetation it supports, the topsoil holds precious moisture in reserve, ready for our use. When the soil is abused or lost through erosion, an invaluable resource may be lost forever. Since our lives depend upon this delicate layer, we all should be concerned about its conservation.

---

1. This paragraph develops one topic, the importance of topsoil, and sticks to that topic. It opens with the topic sentence (underlined).
2. This paragraph uses details to support the topic sentence: importance to all agriculture; dependence of farmers, cattle, trees, and shrubs; water retention.
3. The paragraph is easy to follow. It uses connecting words like *but*, *this*, *when*, and *since* to tie parts of the paragraph together.
4. It has a good beginning. It also has a forceful ending (underlined).
5. For effect, it uses vivid words like *priceless resource*, *fragile skin*, and *delicate layer*.

Exercise 1: Studying a Paragraph

Now study a paragraph by yourself. Be ready to point out how this paragraph displays each of the five characteristics mentioned above.

> For more than a century, stamp collecting has remained a most important hobby for people around the world. Its popularity depends upon certain major appeals. First, stamps are easy to study and store. They take up little space. Second, stamps have many appeals for different people. Some hobbyists collect stamps of one or two countries. Others open their albums to the whole world. Still others collect topics like animals on stamps. Third, stamps are educational. They teach geography, history, economics, art, architecture, current events, and a host of other subjects. Finally, stamps open doors to other nations. Collectors correspond with people in other countries and learn something about how other people live. For all these reasons, stamp collecting has flourished through periods of depression and prosperity, through periods of war and peace.

Exercise 2: Choosing a Topic Sentence

The following paragraph lacks a topic sentence. After you have read the paragraph, follow the directions on page 40.

> In 1987, a child accidentally punched a hole in a wall with a billiard cue. The owners had always assumed the wall was an outside wall, but there was a concealed space beyond. After the owners had stripped away layers of wallpaper they found a small door. There, beyond the door, was a secret compartment left behind by a family more than a century before. Inside the compartment was a bundle of letters. One of the envelopes had been addressed in Natal, South Africa, and sent to Birmingham, England. The stamps on the cover exhibited a rare error, a lack of perforation between the upper and lower stamps in a block of four. The discovery was estimated to be worth more than $5,000.

Write the letter of the best topic sentence.

(*a*) Stamp collecting can be a fascinating hobby.
(*b*) It pays to be persistent, for who knows what may result from sticking to a task?
(*c*) Who knows what treasure may still be found in attics and nooks of old houses?
(*d*) Correspondence between South Africa and England a century ago included some rare stamps.

Your answer: _____

Exercise 3: Eliminating a Sentence That Does Not Belong

Read the following paragraph and follow the directions at the end.

(*a*) In the 19th century, new post offices in the United States often had colorful names. (*b*) As long as a proposed new name didn't conflict with an existing one, it was usually approved by the Post Office Department. (*c*) As a result, new names were unique and colorful. (*d*) At a Massachusetts town meeting to choose a name, everyone had a different idea beginning with "Why not...." (*e*) Because there was no agreement, *Why Not* became the official name. (*f*) A Missouri town submitted a number of names, all of which sounded peculiar. (*g*) *Peculiar* became the name of the town. (*h*) The names of products have unusual origins. (*i*) A California town couldn't agree either, and someone stated it wasn't likely the citizens would ever agree. (*j*) *Likely* became the accepted name. (*k*) A list of unusual names, many of them still in existence, includes *Ordinary*, Virginia; *Bowlegs*, Oklahoma; *Truth or Consequences*, New Mexico; *Chosen*, Florida; *Dime Box*, Texas; *Coarsegold*, California; and *Waterproof*, Louisiana. (*l*) American place-names reflect the hopes and experiences of a bygone day.

Circle the letter of the sentence that does not belong in the paragraph.

a   b   c   d   e   f   g   h   i   j   k   l

Exercise 4: Brainstorming Topics

Look around you. Topics for paragraphs are everywhere. You may have enjoyed a recent television program. The school locker rooms may need repainting. Compact discs may seem to you the entertainment medium of the future. You may predict that the Lakers or Suns or Spurs will win the NBA tournament. You may wonder what the 21st century will bring.

As soon as you get an idea, jot it down. At this stage, don't worry about whether or not it is in good form. Then select one topic and brainstorm all the ideas you can think of about that one topic.

Exercise 5: Developing a Topic

After you have selected one of the topics in your initial list and developed it, write a sound paragraph on that topic. Revise your first draft and develop a finished paragraph.

Exercise 6: Writing a Paragraph

Choose one of the topic sentences listed below and, on the lines that follow, write a paragraph. Follow the suggestions listed previously.

1. When I look for a sport on television, I usually turn to football (baseball, hockey, golf, tennis, or some other).
2. The most satisfactory hobby I know is quilting (coin collecting, woodworking, playing video games, reading, playing the piano, or some other).
3. The importance of a proper diet is becoming increasingly clear.
4. We have owned some unusual pets in the past few years.
5. My favorite month is October (or some other).
6. My favorite type of movie is the thriller (musical, science fiction, comedy, or some other).

_____

_____

_____

_____

_____

_____

_____

_____

_____

_____

_____

_____

Exercise 7

Choose one of the topics listed below and write a paragraph. This time, create your own topic sentence. Follow the suggestions listed previously.

1. My Favorite Meal
2. A Daydream I Often Have
3. My Goal in Life
4. What I Look for in a Friend
5. My Strong Points as a Person
6. My Favorite School Subject
7. A Trip Last Summer
8. A Book I Enjoyed
9. A Television Play I Enjoyed
10. My Favorite News Anchor

_____

_____

_____

_____

_____

_____

_____

_____

_____

_____

_____

_____

5. Writing the Composition to Persuade

Now that you have practiced writing single sentences and paragraphs, you are ready for a longer assignment—the full-length composition. On competency tests, you are often asked to write a composition of about 200 words. You may be asked to persuade someone to agree with you, to think in a certain way, to change a current procedure. You will be given certain specific instructions for doing so. Let's examine the longer composition.

The good longer composition has many of the characteristics of a good paragraph.

Characteristics of Good Compositions

1. A good composition develops a topic at greater length than a paragraph does.
2. A good composition has a point of view and sticks to it.
3. A good composition is aware of the audience for which it is written.
4. A good composition doesn't waste words, avoiding padding and unnecessary details (pages 17–20).
5. A good composition is clear, avoiding confusion and ambiguity (pages 20–25).
6. A good composition hangs together, using the right connecting words to join parts and correctly express relationships (pages 21–23).
7. A good composition chooses strong, effective, specific words to give life to the writing (pages 23–25).
8. A good composition demonstrates sound English structure, without sentence fragments or run-ons (pages 128–142).
9. A good composition is correctly written, free of errors in grammar, usage, and spelling (pages 122–201).
10. A good composition is enjoyable to read or listen to.

How a Composition Is Written

Let's follow a composition from start to finish. Here is a typical composition assignment.

Directions: Write a composition in which you try to persuade a local television station to change its programming. Read *all* the information carefully before you start to write.

Situation: You feel school news is not reported promptly enough. You think the local station, WEXZ, should devote five minutes of its nightly newscast to school news, such as announcements of coming school events.

Your task: Write a composition of about 200 words persuading the managers of WEXZ to include five minutes of school news in the nightly newscast. Give two reasons to support your opinion. Explain each reason.

In your composition be sure to:

- Keep in mind that you are persuading the managers of the television station to act as you suggest.

- State your opinion clearly.

- Give the managers of the television station *two* reasons for your opinion.

- *Explain* each of your two reasons fully.

- Organize what you write.

There is the task. How should you begin? The first stage in the writing process is prewriting. This includes all your planning before you begin to write the first draft. Ordinarily when you decide to write, you must search for a topic. On a competency test, however, the topic is given to you. Of course, you must still do the planning.

Brainstorming

As you have discovered, a good way to start the ball rolling is to brainstorm your ideas.

Here are some things that might occur to you in brainstorming the preceding topic. These ideas are numbered to help in referring to them later.

1. Benefits for school
2. Benefits for station
3. Nightly news at a convenient time
4. Five-minute segment helpful
5. Importance of WEXZ to community
6. Students and parents a large portion of the community
7. Interest of other adults
8. Local news often negative
9. School newspaper only every two weeks
10. School newspaper and television news
11. Announcements not up-to-date
12. Also help future students of Jefferson High School
13. School news would be positive
14. Information about school events, programs, goals
15. Television sometimes has plays about school life
16. Not enough television news about Jefferson High

Where do you go from here? First, look back at the task. If the composition is to have about 200 words, you'll probably need four paragraphs. The first will introduce the topic. The second will give one of the reasons. The third will give the other reason. The fourth will restate the topic.

Writing the First Paragraph

Which numbers in the list might be used in paragraph 1? Number 5 looks like a good sentence to begin with.

> Television station WEXZ is an important force in our community.

Number 16 looks like a good source for two follow-up sentences, for it helps to introduce the coming argument.

> It provides information for all groups of our population, but it is lacking in one important area. It does not give enough news about Jefferson High School, even though the high school is an important part of the community.

Number 4 provides the idea for a sentence that states your main argument.

> I would like to suggest two reasons why I believe a five-minute segment of the local news each evening should be devoted entirely to school news.

There you have your first paragraph. Let's look at it put together.

THE INTRODUCTION

Television station WEXZ is an important force in our community. It provides information for all groups of our population, but it is lacking in one important area. It does not give enough news about Jefferson High School, even though the high school is an important part of the community. I would like to suggest two reasons why I believe a five-minute segment of the local news each evening should be devoted entirely to school news.

Now that's a pretty good paragraph. It introduces the topic. It gets readers interested by talking about a gap and a way to fill the gap. It uses connecting words like *it*, *but*, and *even though*. But this is only the first paragraph. Where do you go from here?

Writing Paragraph 2

A clue to the contents of the next two paragraphs is in the statement, "I would like to suggest two reasons. . . ." That means you'll devote one paragraph to one reason and one to another. But what two reasons can you think of? The brainstorming has suggested a good breakdown. Numbers 1 and 2 provide a good division: benefits for the school and benefits for the station.

Let's take number 1 first. Here's a good paragraph opener.

First, such a segment would benefit our school and its students.

This is a good topic sentence for the second paragraph. Now you must find notes that show such benefits. Number 9 provides a good follow-up to number 1. Here's the sentence that uses this note.

Although we do have a school newspaper, it appears only every two weeks.

Why is this a disadvantage? Another sentence explains.

During that two-week period, most of the news gets stale.

Number 11 provides another follow-up sentence.

At present, important announcements about coming events cannot be kept up-to-date.

At this point, restating your suggestion adds punch to your argument.

A nightly five-minute segment would keep students and their parents informed.

Number 12 suggests an idea for the paragraph's concluding sentence.

It would enrich the lives of present students and give future students a glimpse of what high school is like.

What does the second paragraph look like when assembled?

PARAGRAPH 2

First, such a segment would benefit our school and its students. Although we do have a school newspaper, it appears only every two weeks. During that two-week period, most of the news gets stale. At present, important announcements about coming events cannot be kept up-to-date. A nightly five-minute segment would keep students and their parents informed. It would enrich the lives of present students and give future students a glimpse of what high school is like.

Writing Paragraph 3

The second paragraph has developed the idea of benefits to the *school*. The third paragraph will develop the idea of benefits to the *station*.

Number 2 suggests the topic sentence for paragraph 3.

Second, such a segment would benefit the station.

Numbers 6 and 7 suggest the follow-up sentence.

Students, their parents, and other citizens interested in school life are a large portion of your listeners.

Number 8 suggests a good opening for your major argument.

Much local news here, and around the country, is devoted to negative events, like accidents, robberies, and murders.

Number 13 suggests the right contrast.

I feel sure that five minutes could be taken from these unhappy news reports and devoted to something positive.

Notice how the preceding sentence restates the five-minute idea and ends the paragraph on a strong note. What does the third paragraph look like?

PARAGRAPH 3

> Second, such a segment would benefit the station. Students, their parents, and other citizens interested in school life are a large portion of your listeners. Much local news here, and around the country, is devoted to negative events, like accidents, robberies, and murders. I feel sure that five minutes could be taken from these unhappy news reports and devoted to something positive.

Writing Paragraph 4

You have presented your arguments, but now you must provide a concluding paragraph. This paragraph should urge the station managers to adopt your suggestion. It should also include a very brief summary of your two reasons. To see what the fourth paragraph, with help from number 4, might look like, see the next page.

THE CONCLUSION

> I hope that you will seriously consider this suggestion. I feel that a change of this kind would enlarge your audience and also help keep our young people informed about our school events, programs, and goals.

As you look back, you notice that you have not used numbers 3, 10, and 15. Brainstorming produces items that seem acceptable at first but do not quite fit when the composition is written. Just disregard these items. When you come to the notes used for writing reports, however (pages 93–101), then you must use every item. What does the complete composition look like? Here it is in its entirety.

THE COMPLETE COMPOSITION

Gentlemen:

Television station WEXZ is an important force in our community. It provides information for all groups of our population, but it is lacking in one important area. It does not give enough news about Jefferson High School, even though the high school is an important part of the community. I would like to suggest two reasons why I believe a five-minute segment of the local news each evening should be devoted entirely to school news.

First, such a segment would benefit our school and its students. Although we do have a school newspaper, it appears only every two weeks. During that two-week period, most of the news gets stale. At present, important announcements about coming events cannot be kept up-to-date. A nightly five-minute segment would keep students and their parents informed. It would enrich the lives of present students and give future students a glimpse of what high school is like.

Second, such a segment would benefit the station. Students, their parents, and other citizens interested in school life are a large portion of your listeners. Much local news here, and around the country, is devoted to negative events, like accidents, robberies, and murders. I feel sure that five minutes could be taken from these unhappy news reports and devoted to something positive.

I hope that you will seriously consider this suggestion. I feel that a change of this kind would enlarge your audience and also help keep our young people informed about our school events, programs, and goals.

Let's look back for a moment. What special qualities does this longer composition have?

1. This composition does more than a paragraph can do. It develops an argument at greater length.
2. It has a consistent point of view. It states the case for devoting part of the evening news to school affairs.
3. The composition attempts to persuade the managers of a local television station to change their programming. It is clearly addressed to those individuals and makes clear why a change would be to the station's benefit.
4. The composition hangs together. It uses important signal words like *first* and *second*. It uses other connecting words like *but*, *although*, and *at present*.
5. The composition does not bring in unnecessary details. It states its case and then stops.
6. The composition is free of errors in grammar and usage.

Exercise 1: Studying a Composition

Now study a composition by yourself. Be ready to point out how this composition displays each of the characteristics mentioned above.

Situation: The school board is considering the twelve-month school-year plan. Under this plan, the school building would be kept open during the entire year. Students would continue to have two months' vacation, but groups of students would have their vacations at different times.

Your task: Decide whether you agree or disagree with the suggestion to adopt a twelve-month plan. Write a composition of about 200 words persuading the school board to adopt your point of view. Give two reasons to support your opinion. Explain each reason.

In your composition be sure to:

- Keep in mind that you are trying to persuade the school board, not other students.

- State your opinion clearly.

- Give the school board *two* reasons for your opinion.

- *Explain* each of your two reasons fully.

- Organize what you write.

MODEL COMPOSITION

I wish to add my voice to those voices that support the twelve-month school year. I think this is one of the most creative ideas I've ever heard. It is an idea that in the long run benefits nearly everybody. I'd like to suggest two reasons why I think this plan should be adopted.

First, it benefits students. Under the plan, the total amount of vacation time would not be affected. Vacations would, however, come at different times of the year. Students would have an opportunity to experience periods of rest during spring, fall, and winter. For example, students could enjoy winter sports. All three seasons provide advantages that are lost during the long hot summer. Air-conditioned rooms make school in summer a pleasant experience. The change from the old routines would be refreshing.

Second, it benefits the school system. It uses the school buildings at capacity. Now the schools stand idle for two months. During the summer period, the buildings must be maintained, even though they are empty. The twelve-month program might even eliminate the need for building a new school. With all the economies gained by the change, the schools could afford many needed programs and materials.

A new idea tends to be resisted. Change is often looked upon as bad just because it calls for new methods. I think the twelve-month school year is an idea whose time has come. I hope you will support the idea and put our schools out in front.

Exercise 2: Developing a Point of View

Select three of the following topics. Take a point of view and for each topic tell the two reasons you would give to support your point of view. Direct your composition:

> to a parent telling why you need the family car
> to a friend telling why you think he or she should visit you at Christmas
> to the school principal recommending a new subject for the curriculum
> to the editor of the school newspaper telling why a certain feature should be added
> to a local public official requesting a new traffic light
> to a local TV station asking that a program be retained
> to a manufacturer suggesting improvements in his or her product

Exercise 3: Writing a Composition to Persuade

Directions: Write a composition in which you try to persuade the school cafeteria staff to act in accordance with your suggestion below. Read *all* the information before you start to write.

Situation: There are long lines in the cafeteria. Frequently, you have wanted to go back on line for a snack after finishing your lunch. Yet the long lines and the short time for lunch have prevented you.

Your task: Persuade the school cafeteria staff to install coin machines for dispensing foods to supplement the lunchroom food. These machines would sell raisins, dried apricots, nuts, seeds, and other wholesome snacks. Give two reasons to support your opinion. Explain each reason.

In your composition be sure to:

- Keep in mind that you are trying to persuade the members of the cafeteria staff, not other students.

- State your opinion clearly.

- Give the members of the staff *two* reasons for your opinion.

- *Explain* each of your two reasons fully.

- Organize what you write.

Exercise 4: Writing a Composition from Start to Finish

Select a topic you are interested in, a point of view that you would like others to consider. It may be a personal topic: "Why I Think I Should Have the Family Car for a Coming Dance." This topic might be directed to a parent. It may be a more general topic: "Why I Think Our State Should (or Should Not) Have a Lottery." This topic might be presented as a letter to the editor (pages 82–83). Brainstorm your ideas and then write your first draft in accordance with the suggestions on pages 1–10. Revise the draft and write and proofread the finished copy. Present your composition to its proper audience.

6. Writing the Composition to Explain

The composition to persuade and the composition to explain are first cousins. They sometimes overlap. Persuasion, for example, usually contains explanation. If you are trying to persuade your parents to allow you to drive the family car, you must explain why you deserve the privilege.

You probably use some form of explanation many times a day. "How do you make a carrot cake?" "How do you train a dog to give you its paw?" "Have you ever made a birdhouse? What materials do you use?" "How do a speedometer and an odometer work?" "How does a solar eclipse differ from a lunar eclipse?" "How does a harpsichord differ from a piano?" Answers to questions like these are explanations.

Writing Clear, Complete Definitions

Basic to any explanation is defining. You can't explain a lunar eclipse unless you define *eclipse*. You can't talk about a harpsichord without defining the word. A definition has two major elements: (1) the class the object or event belongs to and (2) the characteristics that distinguish it from others in the same class.

Word	*Class*	*Special Qualities*
An *adze*	is a cutting tool	with the thin arched blade set at right angles to the handle.
A *coloratura*	is a soprano	with a light voice specializing in vocal trills and runs.

Sometimes a synonym provides a definition shortcut. *Frangipani* is a tropical shrub. A *glengarry* is a Scottish woolen cap. *Colossal* means huge. A *Fräulein* is an unmarried girl in German.

A good definition has these characteristics:

1. It is accurate, specific, and complete.
2. The class is the same part of speech as the word itself.
3. The name of the class follows *is* or *means*.
4. The definition is simpler than the original word.
5. It doesn't reuse the word being defined.

Exercise 1: Analyzing Definitions

Three of the following definitions are sound. Three are not. Point out the unsound definitions and tell why they are unhelpful.

1. A homburg is a man's felt hat with a soft, dented crown and a shallow, slightly rolled brim.
2. A pyramid is a huge structure that is found in Egypt near the Nile.

3. A cygnet is a young swan.
4. A turban is a hat.
5. A plurality is when you have more votes than your opponent.
6. Arbitration is the settling of disputes by appeal to an objective impartial party.

_____

_____

_____

Exercise 2: Writing Definitions

Write definitions of three of the following words. Give the class and the particular qualities as suggested on page 52. Use a dictionary if you wish.

abracadabra	bonsai	embitter	lionize
absolute zero	boomerang	epitaph	nose cone
authorize	buoyant	heat lightning	paisley
baritone	centenarian	juror	repetitively
Bedouin	crow's nest	kingfisher	trampoline

_____

_____

_____

_____

_____

_____

How to Write a Good Explanation

1. Decide on who your readers will be. Your explanation to a child will differ from your explanation to an adult.
2. Put yourself in your reader's place. Try to anticipate things that may confuse or puzzle your reader.
3. Connect your explanation with what your reader already knows. Use comparisons and examples.
4. If you must use a technical term, explain it.
5. Don't assume because you know something that your reader will also know it.
6. Use diagrams and charts if they will make your explanation clearer.
7. Be complete and thorough. Don't leave anything out. Leaving out baking powder in a cake mix may ruin the cake.
8. Use connecting words to make your writing smoother.
9. Stick to the topic.
10. Review Section 5, especially ''Characteristics of Good Compositions'' on page 43.

Practice 1: Analyzing Explanations

Why do a clock's hands move in the direction we call *clockwise* instead of in the opposite direction? Read the following pair of explanations and answer the questions at the end.

1

In baseball, skating, and most footraces, the athletes run counterclockwise. Yet traditionally, the hands of a clock move in the opposite direction, or clockwise. Why? The answer probably lies in the history of timekeeping. Before there were clocks, there were sundials. If you have ever watched the shadow of the sun move around the sundial, you recall that the shadow moved in what we now call the *clockwise direction*. When mechanical clocks were devised, what could be more natural than to imitate the shadow of the sun as it moved around the dial? The direction took its name from the clock itself and is called *clockwise*, or *the way the hands of the clock move*. Of course, if clocks had been invented in the Southern Hemisphere, ''clockwise'' would probably be in the opposite direction. Below the equator, the sun's shadow moves counterclockwise.

2

Why do the hands of a clock move opposite to the way most races are run? Naturally, the hands move clockwise. For an explanation of this situation, one should study the history of timekeeping. Before there were clocks, there were water clocks, or clepsydras. There were candle clocks and hourglasses. All of these had serious defects. The sundial, however, is a useful and accurate timepiece if the sun is shining. The clockwise direction is related to the sundial. South of the equator, the shadow of the sun moves opposite to the way the shadow moves in the Northern Hemisphere. Perhaps the hands of our clocks would now move differently if clocks had been invented in the Southern Hemisphere. Nowadays, electric clocks, quartz clocks, and atomic clocks are far more accurate timekeepers than any of their predecessors.

---

1. Which explanation seems clearer?

_____

2. What specific defects does the inferior explanation display?

_____

_____

_____

Exercise 3: Analyzing Explanations

Why are traffic signals arranged as they are? Read the following pair of explanations and answer the questions at the end. (Suggested answers appear at the end of this section on page 60. You may wish to compare your answers to them. Don't peek until you have written your answers!)

1

Color-blind individuals may have trouble with traffic lights. It is difficult for some people to distinguish between red and green. Some red traffic signals have some orange in them, and some green signals have some blue in them. These blends make it easier for the color-blind to tell the difference. Also the placement of the lights has been designed to help the color-blind, who might otherwise be at a great disadvantage.

2

Signals used on railroads probably were the inspiration for the traffic signals we are familiar with today. Red and green signaled *Stop* or *Go*, and we still abide by those colors. Until the 1950s, many traffic signals were displayed horizontally rather than vertically, but this arrangement has generally been abandoned. Nowadays the red signal is placed at the top to help color-blind individuals who might be confused by different layouts. On some traffic signals, the red signal is somewhat larger as an additional help to the color-blind.

---

1. Which explanation seems clearer?

_____

2. What specific defects does the inferior explanation display? Review the practice exercise before you answer.

_____

_____

_____

Exercise 4: Writing an Explanation

Study the following assignment to write an explanation, as well as the sample explanation itself.

Directions: Write an explanation, using the suggestions below.

Situation: For a classroom project, you have been asked to write a how-to explanation. All explanations will be gathered into a class booklet entitled *Our How-to Book.*

Your task: Select one of the following topics and write a clear, concise explanation for the class booklet. Before you begin, brainstorm your ideas. Get as many thoughts down as rapidly as you can.

> How to Park a Car
> How to Make a Sundial
> How to Play Trivial Pursuit (or another board game)
> How to Start Azalea Cuttings
> How to Begin a Stamp Collection
> How to Attract Birds
> How to Be a Baby-Sitter
> How to Read a Weather Map
> How to Build a Simple Bookcase
> How to Make a Cherry Pie (or some other dessert)
> How to Keep Score in Bowling
> How to String a Tennis Racket
> How to Draw a Cartoon
> How to Plan Television Viewing
> How to Make a Good Breakfast Cereal
> How to Take Care of Tropical Fish or a Parakeet
> How to Run a Garage Sale
> How to Program a VCR Efficiently
> How to Schedule a TV Viewing Program for a Week
> How to Make a Flower Arrangement
> How to Start a Terrarium
> How to . . . (Choose your own topic.)

Sample Explanation

> How can you make a good breakfast cereal? If you find breakfast the least attractive meal of the day and most prepared breakfast cereals boring, you'll enjoy making your own cereal. With a little ingenuity and some sound ingredients, you can make a nourishing, tasty cereal that will have the rest of your family clamoring for more. There's another plus. The current interest in low-cholesterol diets, even for young people, suggests avoidance of foods high in cholesterol. This cereal is one good answer.

Although oatmeal is the basis of this supercereal, you should gather together as many of the following ingredients as possible: oat bran, regular (not instant) oatmeal, wheat germ, seven-grain cereal, farina, powdered milk, honey, and lowfat milk.

Take an eight-ounce measuring cup. Into it, put one tablespoon of oat bran, which is highly recommended in all low-cholesterol diets. Add a tablespoon each of wheat germ, seven-grain cereal, and farina. Then fill the eight-ounce cup to the halfway mark with regular oatmeal. Put this mixture into a saucepan. Add two tablespoons of powdered milk and stir the mixture until the ingredients are well mixed. Fill the eight-ounce cup with hot water and pour it into the saucepan. You may add a dash of salt and some raisins. Other dried fruit, like an apricot, a peach, a fig, or a prune, may also be cut into small pieces and added.

Substitutions may, of course, be made. Wheat bran may be substituted for the seven-grain cereal, the farina, or the wheat germ. Such substitutions do not affect the result. The delicious taste and creamy consistency of the mixture please nearly all, even breakfast haters.

The cooked mixture is put into a dish. For sweetening, honey is especially good, but sugar is also acceptable. Milk, preferably low-fat, is added. This cereal may also be served with cream. Unfortunately, the cereal with cream is not a low-cholesterol dish. Adding it defeats part of the purpose of the cereal. The powdered milk, added during the cooking, does give the cereal a creamy taste.

If you put these ingredients together and cook as directed, you may never want any other breakfast again!

Look back for a moment. What special qualities does this sample explanation have?

1. It addresses itself directly to you, the reader. It is pitched to someone of high school age.
2. It provides, at the beginning, a list of ingredients.
3. It takes you step-by-step through the procedure, from measuring to cooking.
4. It is light in tone, in keeping with the classroom project's purpose.
5. It ties in the explanation with a current health topic: the importance of keeping cholesterol levels low.
6. It is smoothly written, with connecting words like *then*, *however*, and *unfortunately*.
7. It provides an explanation that readers can actually put into practice.

Exercise 5

Using the directions for Exercise 4, try your hand at an explanation. Under *Your task*, various topics have been suggested; but if you are stumped, you may choose a topic of your own. Select a topic that you are familiar with and that will interest your fellow students.

First try brainstorming to stimulate your thinking. Next try freewriting, getting your thoughts down as rapidly as possible. Then write your rough draft and revise it. For further help, a classmate and you could exchange revised drafts. As you read each other's work, look for correct definitions and clear explanations. Finally, produce your finished copy, proofread it, and present it to the appropriate audience.

Giving Directions

"Take the first turn to your right, or is it the second? No, it's the first. After you make a right turn, go two or three traffic lights and make a sharp left. I think there's a gas service station on the corner. Or maybe it's a grocery."

Giving good directions is not easy. Many a poor traveler goes miles out of his or her way because someone left out an important direction. A turn at the second traffic light may get the traveler to the destination. A turn at the third traffic light may send the traveler to the next county.

How to Write Good Directions

1. Whenever possible, provide the address and telephone number of the destination.
2. Be accurate, exact, and specific in your directions.
3. Put yourself in your reader's place. What is simple, easy, and obvious to you may be puzzling to your reader.
4. Don't leave anything out. Indicate all left and right turns, and mention landmarks along the way.
5. Keep your directions up-to-date. Signs change. Buildings are torn down. New traffic lights are installed. Last month's directions may be out-of-date today.
6. Write smoothly, using connectives where possible.
7. If a diagram or a map will help, provide it. If possible, indicate distances and compass directions.

Practice 2: Analyzing Directions

"How can I get to Melbourne High School from Melbourne Mall?"

Read the following pair of directions and answer the questions at the end.

1

To get to Melbourne High School from Melbourne Mall, go out onto New Haven Boulevard. This is a pretty wide street, I believe, but there should be traffic lights to help you. After you have driven a while, you will want to look for Babcock Street. Babcock Street cuts through the heart of busy Melbourne and is an important connection with Palm Bay, the next city. Oh, yes, Melbourne Mall is a mile from I-95.

Turn onto Babcock Street. I'm not sure how wide Babcock is at this point, but it always has a lot of traffic. You will then drive past several shopping malls. I believe these malls have a Publix store, a Montgomery Ward, a Sears, and some food stores whose names I forget. Anyway, you will soon make a right turn to reach the high school.

2

To get to Melbourne High School from Melbourne Mall, turn left onto New Haven Boulevard, also called Route 192. Proceed east on New Haven. After you pass the municipal golf course, look for a major intersection with traffic lights. This is Babcock Street. You will recognize it because there are service stations on three corners and a church on the fourth.

Turn left onto Babcock. Proceed past Fee Avenue and Hibiscus Boulevard. As you pass Hibiscus Boulevard, you will find a shopping plaza on your right. Be alert. The next street is Bulldog Lane. An overhead sign identifies that street. Turn right onto it. You have arrived. Melbourne High School is at the corner of Babcock Street and Bulldog Lane. (If you need further help, the school telephone number is 723-4151.)

1. Which set of directions seems clearer?

   _____

2. What errors does the inferior set of directions make? Be specific.

   _____

   _____

   _____

   _____

Exercise 6: Writing Directions

Directions: Now try writing directions of your own. Use the suggestions on how to write good directions as a guide.

Situation: A friend has asked for directions to your house from some other part of town.

Your task: Write the directions for your friend. Add a map if possible. In your composition, be sure to follow the rules for good explanations. Don't take anything for granted.

Model Answers to Exercise 3, page 55

1. Paragraph 2 is preferable. It gives a brief history of traffic signals, an interesting introduction.
2. Paragraph 1 is inferior for these reasons:
    (*a*) It is poorly organized. It doesn't follow a clear pattern.
    (*b*) It mentions the placement of lights but doesn't explain what it is.

7. Writing the Composition to Tell a Story (Narration)

In the Appalachian Mountains, even today, an honored place is held by the storyteller. When mountain folk get together for square dancing, clogging, fiddling, and old-timey music, they also look forward to their favorite storytellers. There are even contests for these talented people.

Not everyone likes persuasion, exposition, or description, but just about everyone loves a good story. If there is a universal need, it seems to be for good narrative. In most libraries, mysteries, westerns, and science fiction have shelves all to themselves. They are always popular because they depend upon good stories. You can hold your listeners by a good story, either spoken or written.

Telling an Anecdote

An anecdote is a story in little. It is a compressed account of an interesting, often amusing, incident. Being brief, it packs much information into little space.

Practice: Comparing Anecdotes

Read the following two anecdotes and answer the questions on page 62.

1

Mozart was a composer who was a prodigy as a child and in his brief life, despite his youth, he created an incredible number of masterpieces. Once he was stopped by a young person who had a question for Mozart and asked him how he, the speaker, might be able to write a symphony. Mozart told the young man that since he was still very young, he might begin by writing ballads, but the hopeful composer pointed out that Mozart himself had composed symphonies when he was young, in fact only ten years old. Mozart replied that he didn't ask *how*.

2

Mozart was a child prodigy who created a number of masterpieces in his brief life. Once a young person asked him how to write a symphony.

"You're a very young man," said Mozart. "Why not begin with ballads?"

The would-be composer said, "Yes, but *you* composed symphonies when you were only ten."

"Ah," replied Mozart, "but I didn't ask *how*!"

1. Which narrative is more interesting?

   _____

2. How does dialogue help the narrative?

   _____

   _____

3. How does one of the narratives compress ideas to help the flow?

   _____

   _____

   _____

   _____

   _____

How to Tell a Story Effectively

1. Decide on who your readers will be. Telling a story to a contemporary is different from telling the same story to a grandparent.
2. Review the suggestions on pages 1–10.
3. Start briskly, without wasting time on what happened earlier. Be concise and economical.
4. Select the best part of your story, not the entire episode. Concentrate on that part.
5. Don't give away the climax or point too soon. Save your punchline for later.
6. Bring in description where it advances the story, but don't get bogged down in it (pages 66–69).
7. Use dialogue where possible to brighten the narrative and move it along. Review the correct punctuation of quotations (pages 179–180).
8. End with strength. Leave your readers with a feeling of satisfaction. Don't trail off weakly.

Exercise 1: Writing a Brief Anecdote

Try your hand at writing a brief anecdote, following the suggestions above. Brainstorm some possible topics, or use one of the following to prime the pump.

A friend's humorous experience
An incident involving a celebrity
A story based on a historical character
An unusual episode in your own life

Telling a Personal Experience

You probably have a favorite story to tell about something that happened to you. It is longer than an anecdote; but like an anecdote, it tells a tale someone will enjoy listening to.

Exercise 2: Studying a Personal Narrative

Read the following account of a personal experience and point out how it follows the suggestions for writing narratives.

With great anticipation, we four hardy hikers started climbing the Huntington Ravine Trail on the slope of Mt. Washington in New Hampshire's White Mountains. The early section, shared with the Tuckerman Ravine Trail, is gently graded and easy to master.

"This isn't as bad as I expected," my friend Ted said, and we all agreed.

Gradually, though, the climbing became steeper and the trail narrower. Up and up we went, zigzagging back and forth, hugging the side of the ravine, rising higher and higher above timberline. Then ahead of us lay the most challenging part of the hike.

"Is this the famous cliff crossover?" asked Ann.

I looked at the narrow ledge, with its very slight foothold, and said, with some misgivings, "This must be it. It looks pretty scary!"

There was a slight indentation on the side of the granite cliff. The cliff itself faced us at a 45-degree angle, with just that small shelf for crossing. Then the slope fell off sharply from the meager trail.

"Let me go first," Marie bravely suggested, and off she went, picking her way carefully so as not to slip down the sharp slope. Ann went next, calling back, "Come on. It was great!"

Then Ted, putting on a show of bravado but secretly concerned, inched across the trail.

"Always room for one more," said Ted, relieved that he had managed the crossing.

With my friends so courageously across, I gathered myself together . . . and made it.

"That was great!" said Marie.

"Yes, but let's go back down by another trail," I suggested.

My companions didn't disagree. We all sat huddled in a sheltered nook and congratulated ourselves on our bravery. As we were sitting there, catching our breaths and readying ourselves for the remaining climb to the top of the ravine, we heard a series of shouts. Then there passed us, tripping merrily along and laughing at their private jokes, a troop of very young girl hikers from a camp in the valley. As we looked in bafflement and some dismay, the last little girl skipped happily and unconcernedly across the dreaded ledge and joined the rest of her group, now 30 yards up the trail.

Our amazing exploit had shrunk a bit, and we felt sheepish, but we resolutely put on our backpacks and trudged upward.

Exercise 3: Writing a Personal Narrative

Study the following assignment to write a narrative. For help in completing this assignment, use the previous example and the suggestions on page 62.

Directions: Write a personal-experience narrative, using the suggestions below.

Situation: Your class is preparing a booklet to amuse and entertain members of a nearby nursing home. The title of the booklet is ''That's What Happened to Us.''

Your task: By first brainstorming ideas and limiting the topic and then writing rough and final drafts, tell a story. If one of the following does not suggest a topic, provide one of your own.

> When Baby-Sitting Was No Fun
> An Encounter with Poison Ivy
> Lost My Keys
> What Are Friends For?
> Life Doesn't Imitate Television
> It Was No Picnic!
> A City Boy (Girl) in the Country
> When I Sneered at Superstitions
> A Case of Mistaken Identity
> Life's Brightest (or Darkest) Moment
> Who Said I Couldn't Cook!
> There Are Parties and Parties
> Lateness Is Not a Virtue
> A Trip to a Television Studio

Exercise 4: Using a Proverb to Write a Personal Narrative

Have you ever had a personal experience that demonstrates the truth (or falsity) of a proverb? Perhaps ''Lightning never strikes twice in the same place'' suggests the time when you forgot to pick up your baby brother at nursery school—for the second time. Look back at the proverbs on page 13. This time, instead of explaining the proverb, write a personal-experience narrative that illustrates how the proverb is a good title for something that happened to you. Or choose another proverb from the following list. Or choose one of your own. You may be able to use one of the sentences you wrote for Exercise 7 on page 16.

There's no joy in anything unless we share it.
Don't judge a book by its cover.
You can't have your cake and eat it too.
One good turn deserves another.
The grass is always greener on the other side of the fence.
Every dog has his day.
The biter is sometimes bit.
The proof of the pudding is in the eating.
One man's meat is another's poison.
Variety is the spice of life.
There is more than one way out of the woods.
Youth will have its fling.

8. Writing Description

Description often enlivens a narrative, enriches exposition, and adds punch to persuasion. Though it is usually part of a larger project, description by itself can be fun to write and enjoyable to read. Advertisers use description to set forth the merits of their products. Political candidates use description to picture the ideal state of affairs that will follow from their election. In pleas to parents, teenagers use description to picture the advantages of a week's stay at Camp Tonawandah.

Sense Impressions

A basic element in description is the appeal to the senses. An advertiser for a pizza restaurant emphasizes the rich red tomato sauce, the crisp crust, the tangy spices, and the creamy mozzarella cheese. On television, the ad shows a slice of pizza with strings of cheese dangling from the first bite. Appeals to all five senses sell products and prove that description can be a major ingredient of effective persuasion.

Practice 1: Studying the Appeal to the Senses

What sense does each of the following sentences primarily appeal to: sight, sound, taste, smell, touch?

_____ 1. As I sank into the new chair, I enjoyed the velvety feel of the fabric.

_____ 2. The low murmur of bees contrasted with the shrill cawing of some crows overhead.

_____ 3. The earthy fragrance of the greenhouse was combined with the faint odor of the first hyacinths.

_____ 4. At Thanksgiving, I particularly like the slightly bittersweet tang of the cranberry sauce, especially when it is combined with the bland turkey.

_____ 5. The acrobat lunged into space, did a double somersault, and then, with arms outstretched, grasped the waiting arms of the catcher.

_____ 6. Suddenly, without warning, all the lights in our area went out, and the normally brilliantly lighted street was bathed only in a pale moonlight.

_____ 7. I left the warm locker room, dashed out into the bitter cold, and then gratefully dived into the hot springs.

_____ 8. The school lunchroom is an unmelodic combination of clattering dishes, scraping chairs, and enthusiastic students all talking at once.

_____ 9. The bakery kitchen blended the aroma of baking bread with traces of dill, basil, and chocolate.

_____ 10. I took a forkful of salad and experienced suddenly a sour, sharp encounter with a vinegar-and-oil dressing that had omitted the oil.

How to Describe Effectively

1. Try to decide who your readers will be and tilt your description toward their interests.
2. Use vivid sense words to help your reader share your experience.
3. Choose the important points. Provide enough details to draw your picture effectively, but don't overwhelm the reader with trivia. Be selective.
4. Decide on the order to follow. After you have chosen your viewpoint, don't jump around. Go from left to right, for example, but don't lose your reader in a confusion of ''on the left,'' ''on the right,'' ''on the left.''
5. Use connecting words to show the relationships more clearly.
6. Review ''Characteristics of Good Compositions'' on page 43.

Exercise 1: Analyzing a Description

Read the following description and point out how it follows the suggestions for writing description.

> Since our plans included a hike up the dramatic cone of Mt. Adams, we started on the King Ravine Trail. Several miles into the hike, at the foot of the ravine, we burst upon an area called Mossy Fall. It was like an enchanted amphitheater. The delicious odor of balsam filled the air, and a cool breeze caressed our heated skins. The only sounds were the slight soughing of the wind in the trees and the rhythmic splatter of water on rocks.
>
> The falls, about six feet high and a dozen feet wide, dominated the scene. To the left of the falls, the trail continued on its way, winding upward, inviting hikers to sample the vistas that lay ahead. The falls themselves, center stage, looked like a scene from _The Wizard of Oz_, qualifying as part of the Emerald City. Though our own Yellow Brick Road had been paved with brown pine needles, it had taken us to this mysterious glen. The falls were almost entirely covered in green. The moss was everywhere. Some of it in the water, slightly larger than the rest, waved ceaselessly in the steady flow, even at the very top of the falls. Rocks here and there broke the pattern of the flowing water and caused an endless variation of little streams and miniature falls. At the right side

of the falls, just below the restless cataract, there was a quiet pool. Water striders skimmed along the surface. Only occasionally was a streamlet diverted to ruffle for a moment the uncanny stillness of this pool so close to an area of raging motion.

We couldn't resist the temptation. We took off boots and socks and dangled our feet in the icy water. Though our feet tingled and had to be withdrawn every minute or so, we felt refreshed and knew that our no-longer-tired feet appreciated the stimulation. Reluctantly we put on socks and shoes and left behind this miniature paradise.

Exercise 2: Writing a Description

Study the following assignment. Use the previous example and the suggestions on page 67 for help in writing your description.

Directions: Write a descriptive composition, using the suggestions below.

Situation: Your class is planning to put together a booklet with the general title "Our School."

Your task: Plan to describe a room or other part of your school. Consult with your classmates so that each one takes a different area to describe. As usual, brainstorm your ideas and then write the rough and final drafts. The following may provide some suggestions for choosing.

> The lunchroom
> The gymnasium
> The locker rooms
> The library
> The science laboratory
> The sports field
> The auditorium
> The front of the building
> The home economics room
> The language laboratory
> The computer room
> The room where you have your English (or another) class
> A corridor during change of class
> The school kitchen
> The English (or another) office
> A storeroom
> The main lobby

The Character Sketch

People are always fascinating. Since personalities are so varied and actions often unpredictable, readers enjoy biographies and autobiographies, anecdotes about the famous, thumbnail sketches that reveal striking qualities. An effective descriptive paragraph can capture a major quality and leave a lasting impression of a person.

Practice 2: Analyzing a Character Sketch

The novelist Charles Dickens was a master of the thumbnail sketch. Within the space of a paragraph, he often captured the essential element of a character. In the following description of Miss Murdstone, from *David Copperfield*, Dickens leaves us with a single overriding impression. Read it and answer the questions at the end.

> It was Miss Murdstone who was arrived, and a gloomy-looking lady she was, dark, like her brother, whom she greatly resembled in face and voice; and with very heavy eyebrows, nearly meeting over her large noise, as if, being disabled by the wrongs of her sex from wearing whiskers, she had carried them to that account. She brought with her two uncompromising hard black boxes, with her initials on the lids in hard brass nails. When she paid the coachman she took her money out of a hard steel purse, and she kept the purse in a very jail of a bag which hung upon her arm by a heavy chain, and shut up like a bite. I had never, at that time, seen such a metallic lady altogether as Miss Murdstone was.

1. What essential element about Miss Murdstone does Dickens want us to remember? Is this feeling positive or negative?

_____

_____

2. What descriptive words further that description?

_____

_____

_____

Exercise 3: Writing a Thumbnail Sketch

Using the models and suggestions in this section and the section on paragraphs (pages 38–42), write a thumbnail sketch of a person. It may be a member of your family, a friend, an acquaintance, a celebrity, or even a fictional character. Confine yourself to a single effective paragraph. Try to convey a single impression. As usual, call upon brainstorming to get your ideas on paper quickly. Then, more deliberately, write the rough draft and the final draft. Exchange papers with a classmate. Each reader will try to uncover the major impression intended by the writer.

9. Writing the Personal Essay

How do you feel about child-proof medicine bottles that defy intelligent adults? About weekends with not a thing scheduled? About people who tell you the score of sports events you've taped for later playing? About the collecting bug? About managing a budget? About camping?

You probably have strong opinions about one or more of the questions. Expressing these opinions in a composition can be fun to write and enjoyable to read. The literary form that answers such questions is the personal or familiar essay. Newspaper columnists like Art Buchwald and Irma Bombeck are excellent essayists.

Practice: Analyzing an Essay

Read the following opening paragraphs for an essay on the topic ''Alarm Clocks.'' Answer the questions at the end.

1

There are times when I consider alarm clocks the invention of the devil. I am deep in health-giving sleep when suddenly . . . ''R-r-r-ring!'' The sound is not a gentle suggestion, ''Wake up.'' It really says, ''You'd better get up or I'll blast this siren until you do.'' I open one eye and try to close both ears. Alas, the clock is on a night table beyond my reach. I put one foot on the cold floor, groping for the bed slipper. It's no use. I thrust aside the covers, bravely rush to the clock, have a hard time finding the OFF button in my semiconscious state, and finally get relief from that jangling discord that begins my day. I have suggestions for a better way.

2

Alarm clocks are annoying inventions. In the morning I am awakened by the jangling of the alarm. I'm not eager to get up, so I just wait a moment and hope that the noise will cease. It continues and I decide to turn it off. I can't reach it, however, and so I come to a decision. I will get out of bed and turn off the alarm. To make matters worse, I can't find my bed slippers. As I have already mentioned, I decide to get out of bed. I walk to the table and have difficulty finding the OFF button. The noise stops, and I am happy. Some improvements can be made.

1. Which essay is more interesting?

   _____

   _____

2. What colorful words does the better essay use?

   _____

   _____

3. How do quotations help the flow of the essay?

   _____

   _____

How to Write an Essay Effectively

1. Choose a subject that you have some opinions about.
2. As always, brainstorm your ideas before you begin to write.
3. Arrange your ideas in easy-to-follow order.
4. Use colorful words and vivid details.
5. Keep the treatment light and humorous, if possible.
6. Use quotations freely.
7. Use an informal, conversational style. Let the style express your personality.
8. Picture your reader sitting next to you. Imagine that you are talking to him or her.

Exercise 1: Reading a Personal Essay

Read the following personal essay and point out how it follows the suggestions for writing essays.

Mastering the VCR

One of the greatest inventions of recent history can also be one of the most frustrating. I'm referring to that magical box called the *videocassette recorder*, or VCR for short. The VCR extends our powers, allows us to tape programs while we are out, helps us plan our viewing for maximum effect. To suit our mood or convenience, we can choose the moment for replaying the tape. With the remote control, we can sit comfortably, viewing that detective story we hated to miss. If the British actors speak in a difficult dialect, we can play the difficult section back until we have understood what they have said. If Susie says, ''I'm in love with Humphrey Bogart and *Casablanca*,'' she can watch the movie over and over to her heart's content. The VCR is indeed a miracle.

The miracle does not, however, come without problems. When my parents bought their first VCR many years ago, the task was simple. All the buttons were understandable. The taping was nearly foolproof. Of course, only one program could be taped at any one time. There was no remote. To replay a section, the viewer had to rewind—but without seeing the rewound picture. Still, the task wasn't so difficult.

Simplicity has given way to complexity. There are improvements, like on-screen programing and multiple programing, but there are problems with all those new buttons. From a handful, the number of buttons has increased at least fivefold. The VCR now has more possibilities than ever and is certainly an improved instrument. But there are more challenges than ever.

There is a current story about the VCR owner who learned to play back rented tapes but never mastered the art of taping programs off the air. Whenever he wanted to do so, he called the ten-year-old next door. ''S.O.S.! Please come in and set the tape!'' In my own experience, there are many intelligent adults who look upon the VCR with trepidation, fearful of getting the wrong program, the wrong channel, the wrong time, even the wrong day. Ordinarily they can read directions, but they find the directions provided with the VCR very complicated.

Young people born into the computer age are at home with these technological marvels, but members of the older generation are a little uneasy. I would say to these uncertain souls, ''No household should be without a ten-year-old who can adjust the VCR, run the personal computer, and handle all those extra telephone options.''

Exercise 2: Writing a Personal Essay

Study the following assignment to write a personal essay. For help in completing this assignment, use the previous example and the suggestions on page 71.

Directions: Write a personal essay, using the suggestions below.

Situation: You have been asked to submit a personal essay for possible publication in the school literary magazine.

Your task: Consider some of the subjects you have opinions about. Write a personal essay that illuminates some of your ideas on the subject. The following may provide some suggestions for choosing, but do not be limited by them.

> Litterbugs
> Music I Enjoy
> Roadside Signs
> The Art of Baby-Sitting
> Behavior at the Movies
> Family Reunions
> How to Find a Bargain
> Diets
> Pet Peeves
> Dance Crazes
> Television Commercials
> Fast Food
> Sharing Clothes
> Being the Middle Child
> Dogs I Have Known (cats, gerbils, goldfish . . .)
> The Joys (or agonies) of Travel
> Homework
> Part-Time Work

Exercise 3

"The ghost that got into our house on the night of November 17, 1915, raised such a hullabaloo of misunderstandings that I am sorry I didn't just let it keep on walking, and go to bed."

This is the opening sentence of James Thurber's hilarious essay "The Night the Ghost Got In." Other provocative titles from the collection called *My Life and Hard Times* include "The Night the Bed Fell," "The Day the Dam Broke," and "The Dog That Bit People."

Perhaps you can recall a personal experience that would be fun to tell about. You might title it "The Night That . . . ," "The Day That . . . ," or some other title. Write a personal essay following the suggestions provided earlier. Don't omit the brainstorming stage. It will provide you with many of your ideas. Keep the essay light and humorous.

10. Writing the Business Letter

On a competency test, you may be expected to write a good business letter. It should show correct form and be well written. It should also bear correct punctuation (pages 172–183) and capitalization (pages 184–190).

Correct Form

In addition to the body, the business letter has five parts. Let's examine each in turn. (All names and addresses are fictitious).

Heading

> 15 Barnes Place
> Valley Stream, NY 11580
> October 10, 19--

1. The first line of the heading gives the street address or the post office box number. Do not abbreviate.

2. The second line gives the town or city, state, and ZIP code. The official abbreviation for *New York* is *NY*. If you know the abbreviations of other state names, you may use them. (See page 177.) Otherwise, spell them out.

3. The third line gives the date. Don't abbreviate.

Inside Address

> Barrett's Art Service
> 45 Park Avenue South
> New York, NY 10012

1. The first line of the inside address gives the name of the person or company you are writing to.

2. The second line gives the street address or the post office box number.

3. The third line gives the town or city, state, and ZIP code.

Except for the official state abbreviation, do not abbreviate.

Salutation

```
Gentlemen:
```

The salutation of a business letter ends with a colon (:). Common business-letter salutations include *Dear Ms. Porter, Dear Mr. Jones, Gentlemen.*

Closing

```
Sincerely yours,
```

The closing of a letter ends with a comma (,). The first word only is capitalized. Common business-letter closings include *Yours truly, Sincerely, Very truly yours, Cordially yours.*

Signature

```
Roberto Quesada
```

Roberto Quesada

Try to make your signature as legible as possible. To help your correspondent, type or print your name below your signature.

Now let's put all the parts of a business letter together.

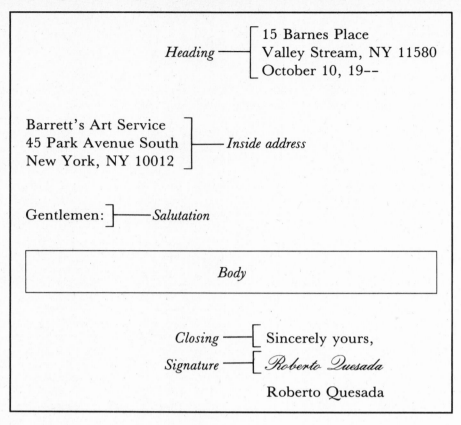

The Envelope

Note the correct form of the envelope:

Roberto Quesada
15 Barnes Place
Valley Stream, NY 11580

Barrett's Art Service
45 Park Avenue South
New York, NY 10012

Practice 1: Studying a Business Letter

Study the following assignment to write a business letter as well as the letter itself on page 78.

Directions: Write a business letter about the situation described below. Read *all* the information before you start to write.

Situation: You sent an order for photographs to Color Photo. The order arrived but it was incomplete. The advertisement promised 24 wallet-sized photographs, three 5 × 7 enlargements, and one 8 × 10 enlargement. You sent $10.75 plus 65¢ for handling and 50¢ for first-class mail return. You received the wallet-sized photographs but not the enlargements.

Your task: Write a business letter about this situation to: Color Photo, P.O. Box 230A. Complete this address by using your own city or town, state, and ZIP code.

In your letter be sure to:

- Explain the situation.

- Explain what you want Color Photo to do for you.

- Give complete and correct information.

- Use an acceptable business-letter form.

20 Partridge Road
El Paso, TX 79910
March 26, 19--

Color Photo
P.O. Box 230A
El Paso, TX 79910

Gentlemen:

On February 18, I sent an order for photos as advertised in *Seventeen*. The advertisement promised 24 wallet-sized photos, three 5 × 7 enlargements, and one 8 × 10 enlargement. In accordance with the directions, I enclosed a photo to be copied and a money order for $11.90 to cover all postage and handling costs.

I received the order yesterday. It contained the wallet-sized photos but not the four enlargements. I am returning the original photo. Will you please make up the enlargements and send them to me as conveniently as possible. Thank you for attending to this matter.

Sincerely yours,

Ellen Franklyn

Ellen Franklyn

Refer to the suggestions in the directions.

1. Note that the letter briefly and clearly explains the situation. It points out that four enlargements had been omitted from the order.

2. Then it explains simply what Color Photo is to do: provide the missing enlargements.

3. Information is complete and accurate. The writer did not forget to send the original photo back.

4. The business-letter form is correct.

Exercise 1: Studying a Business Letter

Now study a business letter by yourself. Be ready to point out how the letter on page 80 meets the requirements of the situation.

Directions: Write a business letter about the situation described below. Read *all* the information before you start to write.

Situation: You sent an order to Johnson Printers for 250 Crystal Clear return-address labels. You sent a money order for $4.48, which covered the cost of the labels and return postage. Six weeks have elapsed, but you have not yet received the order.

Your task: Write a business letter about this situation to: Johnson Printers, 4280 Johnson Building. Complete this address by using your own city or town, state, and ZIP code.

In your letter be sure to:

- Explain the situation.

- Explain what you want Johnson Printers to do for you.

- Give complete and correct information.

- Use an acceptable business-letter form.

19 Northfield Lane
Philadelphia, PA 19104
January 12, 19--

Johnson Printers
4280 Johnson Building
Philadelphia, PA 19104

Dear Sir or Madam:

Six weeks ago, I noticed your advertisement in *Parade* magazine. I sent an order for 250 Crystal Clear return-address labels. I included my full name and address as well as a money order for $4.48, which covered the cost of the labels and the return postage.

Since so much time has passed, I am worried about the order. I'm afraid it may have been lost. Would you check and see that the order is shipped as soon as possible. The heading at the top of this letter gives my correct address for the labels. May I hear from you.

Very truly yours,

Rhoda Berman

Rhoda Berman

Exercise 2: Writing a Business Letter

Directions: Write a business letter about the situation described below. Read *all* the information before you start to write.

Situation: You ordered a book from Publishers United. The book, *Children's Toys and Furniture*, arrived with 48 pages missing.

Your task: Write a business letter about this situation to Publishers United, Box 132, Dept. R2. Ask for directions about returning the damaged book and getting either a new book or a refund. Complete this address by using your own city or town, state, and ZIP code.

In your letter be sure to:

- Explain the situation.

- Explain what you want Publishers United to do for you.

- Give complete and correct information.

- Use an acceptable business-letter form.

Practice 2: Studying a Letter of Application

Study the following assignment to write a letter of application as well as the letter itself on page 82.

Directions: Write a business letter about the situation described below. Read all the information before you start to write.

Situation: Your are interested in getting information from a community college in your area. You are considering making an application to the college.

Your task: Write a business letter to Blue Ridge Community College, Blue Ridge Tech Road, Flat Rock, NC 28731.

In your letter be sure to

- Explain why you seek information.

- Ask for booklets, courses of study, and an application form.

- Give complete and correct information.

- Use an acceptable business-letter form.

309 Fernwood Drive
Hendersonville, NC 28739
February 18, 19--

Blue Ridge Community College
Blue Ridge Tech Road
Flat Rock, NC 28731

Gentlemen:

I am seeking information about community colleges in the Western North Carolina area. Yours is one of the colleges I am most interested in. I have heard you provide courses in journalism. In high school, my major extracurricular interest has been the school newspaper.

Please send me information about the courses of study you offer, with special emphasis on print journalism. I'll be grateful to receive an application form, along with any booklets that will help me to plan my study for the years ahead.

Sincerely,

Sarah Collingsworth

Sarah Collingsworth

Again, refer to the suggestions in the directions.

1. The letter briefly and accurately states the situation.
2. It courteously asks for booklets and other helpful information.
3. The information is complete and accurate.
4. The letter follows acceptable business-letter form.

Exercise 3: Writing a Letter of Application

Choose a local community college or another college you might be interested in. Write a letter of application. Make clear your own interests and request all necessary information.

Exercise 4: Writing a Letter to the Editor

Using correct letter form, write a letter to the editor of your school or local newspaper. Express your point of view about something you approve of or disapprove of. In the letter, suggest some changes that will improve the situation. Review the suggestions (page 43) for writing good compositions. Review ''Writing the Composition to Persuade'' (pages 43–51).

Exercise 5: Writing a Business Letter

Using correct letter form, write a business letter on one of the following topics. If one of these letters reflects a situation in your life, prepare to mail the letter.

1. You have ordered an item, but have not received it.
2. You have not been able to find a particular item in a local department store.
3. You have been asked to pay a bill you have already paid.
4. You have received an item you sent away for repair, but the repair is unsatisfactory.
5. On many occasions, you have been unable to get items on sale at a local store. Suggest the use of ''rain checks.''
6. You have subscribed to a magazine, but have not yet received a copy.
7. You have ordered camping information from Florida's Department of Tourism in Tallahassee, but have not received it.
8. You were promised a free product for sending a coupon, but you have not yet received the product.
9. You have bought a model-boat kit, but several important parts are missing.
10. You have ordered stationery with letterhead imprinted. The order has arrived, but your name is misspelled.

11. Writing the Friendly Letter

Besides the greater informality of a friendly letter, there are a few differences between it and the business letter.

Correct Form

In addition to the body, the friendly letter has four parts. Let's examine each in turn. (All names and addresses are fictitious.)

Heading

> 21 Hilltop Avenue
> Lexington, MA 02173
> February 27, 19--

1. The first line of the heading gives the street address or the post office box number. Do not abbreviate.

2. The second line gives the town or city and state. The official abbreviation for *Massachusetts* is *MA*. If you know the abbreviations of other state names, you may use them. (See page 177.) Otherwise, spell them out.

3. If you are writing to someone who is sure to know the address without checking, you may omit lines 1 and 2.

4. The third line gives the date. Don't abbreviate.

Inside Address

This is customarily omitted in a friendly letter.

Salutation

> Dear Aunt Laura,

The salutation of a friendly letter ends with a comma (,). Common friendly-letter salutations include *Dear Tammy, Dear Grandmother, Dear Miss Juarez, Dear Mr. and Mrs. Girard.*

Closing

Your niece,

The closing of a friendly letter ends with a comma (,). The first word is capitalized. Common friendly letter closings include *Your nephew, Your pen pal, Affectionately yours, Love, As ever, Sincerely, Till Friday.*

Signature

Margo

Try to make your signature as legible as possible. The last name is, of course, unnecessary in corresponding with relatives or close friends. Now let's put all the elements together.

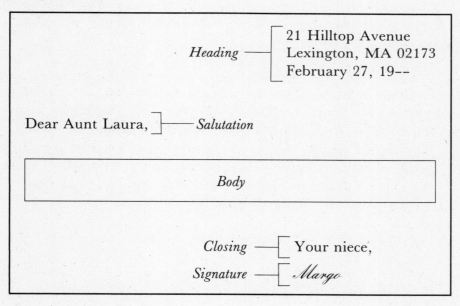

The envelope for the friendly letter is essentially the same as that for the business letter. (See page 76.)

Types of Friendly Letters

There are many types of friendly letters, each with its own special flavor and purpose.

Newsy Letter. This is the most general of all friendly letters. Its purpose is to keep lines of communication open, to keep in touch with friends. Though the newsy letter has been partly taken over by the telephone, it is still an important link between friends, especially those in areas distant from each other. Everyone likes to receive letters. To receive letters, you must also send them.

How to Write a Good Newsy Letter

1. Have your correspondent's previous letter in front of you so that you can respond to questions, comments, and news items.
2. Begin with a bright opening sentence. Avoid such negative comments as "I had nothing to do, so I thought I'd drop you a line."
3. Be as positive as you can. Don't dwell on bad news.
4. Give details as if you were writing a news paragraph: *who*, *what*, *where*, *when*, *why*, and *how*.
5. Write the way you talk. Introduce humor where possible. Looked at in a special way, everyday details are often funny.
6. There are many subjects to talk about: your experiences, unusual adventures, travel and travel plans, hobbies, family, school, afterschool work, books read and movies seen. Television is a good common subject.
7. Share an interesting anecdote or joke, if you have one. Enclose a humorous clipping from a magazine or newspaper.

Exercise 1: Studying a Friendly Letter

Study the following assignment to write a friendly letter. A sample letter is included on pages 87–88.

Directions: Write a friendly letter about the situation described below. Read all the information before you start to write.

Situation: You have just received a letter from a friend whom you haven't seen in several months. He or she has mentioned a trip taken during the summer, has retold some amusing episodes in the school lunchroom, and mentioned several books and television programs enjoyed. Your correspondent has closed with "Hope to hear from you soon."

Your task: Reply to this letter. Imagine it has been received from one of your actual friends.

In your letter be sure to:

- Follow the how-to guide on this page.

- Comment on things mentioned in your correspondent's letter.

- Provide some interesting news of your own.

- Mention a television program or book you have especially enjoyed.

- Use correct friendly-letter form.

Sample Newsy Letter

2190 South Beverly Street
Los Angeles, CA 90025
September 19, 19--

Dear Jason,

Your welcome letter really brought me up to date on the goings-on around your house. You have certainly been busy the past few months. Your camping trip to Bryce Canyon and Zion National Park sounds like the kind of trip I'd like to take some day. I hope your weather was fine, but then I've heard that weather in those areas is beautiful in August.

The opening of school is not always an easy way to leave the summer behind, but this year all is well. The subjects I'm taking are pretty interesting, and my teachers keep things moving. There have been some amusing spots, too. Our school uses abbreviations like *ST* for *stenography* and *SP* for *Spanish*. One of my friends sat in a stenography class for two weeks before realizing it was not a Spanish class. ''It all seemed a foreign language to me anyway'' was the misplaced student's explanation.

You mentioned that you especially enjoy *Nova* and *Nature* on Public Television stations. I agree. I marvel at the kind of photography that can catch the hatching of a thrush's eggs or the battle between a grasshopper and ants. My favorite nature program was the story of termite mounds in Africa. The camera got inside the mounds and showed how workers tend the queen, how the queen spends all her time laying eggs, and how every termite seems to know its job. The most dramatic scene of all was the fight to the death between a termite soldier and a much larger marauding insect. It was almost a heroic struggle between a valiant knight and a superior opponent. I didn't think I could feel sorry for a dying insect, but I was moved by the heroic, but unequal, battle.

Your trip out West has had me dreaming of our family's planned trip to Acadia National Park in Maine next summer. We hear the water is too cold for swimming, but the mountains are perfect for hiking. I think I prefer camping to any other kind of vacation.

> What discs and tapes have you added recently to your fabulous collection? My parents gave me two music videos for my birthday. Hey, you should have seen my little brother Teddy trying to dance to the music!
>
> We all miss you and hope to see you again at Christmastime.
>
> > Your old pal,
> >
> > *Alex*

Exercise 2: Writing a Friendly Letter

Using the directions, situation, and task from the preceding sample letter, write a newsy letter of your own. Use your home address for the heading. Use the name of a friend or relative for your correspondent. (After the letter has been read, you may wish to send it, or a copy, to the correspondent.)

Letter of Invitation, Acceptance, or Rejection. Like the newsy letter, this letter is often replaced by the telephone call. But there are still occasions when it is courteous and necessary to send a letter of invitation.

How to Write a Letter of Invitation

1. Be complete, clear, and friendly.
2. Give the exact information about date, time, and place.
3. Give plenty of time for the reply.
4. If the letter of invitation is combined with the newsy letter, be sure that the invitation is clear and is not overlooked because it is buried in the body of the letter.

How to Write a Letter of Acceptance or Rejection

1. If you can attend, be prompt in accepting the invitation. Show that you are happy at being invited.
2. For safety's sake, repeat the information about date, time, and place. If necessary, ask for directions.
3. If you cannot attend, give a specific, sincere reason for not attending.
4. Express thanks for being asked.

If you receive a printed card with the words *Regrets only*, you need reply only if you are *not* attending.

Thank-You Letter. If you have received a gift, do not overlook the thank-you letter. The gift-giver appreciates some acknowledgment of the time and thoughtfulness that went into the selection. A related letter is the bread-and-butter letter. It is also a thank-you, usually for having been entertained at someone's house for a weekend or more.

How to Write a Thank-You Letter

1. Mention the gift specifically and suggest how you plan to use it. Even if you dislike the gift, you can commend the thought.
2. If you have stayed with a family for a period, tell what you especially enjoyed during the visit. A separate letter to your friend's parents is a thoughtful touch.
3. Be prompt. If you delay a thank-you letter for a mailed gift, your donor will wonder whether you received the gift.

Congratulations. There are special moments in every life: a graduation, an award, an election, a championship, a unique achievement. Hearing from friends makes the achievement sweeter.

How to Write a Letter of Congratulation

1. Write soon after the achievement.
2. Mention the achievement specifically and indicate your appreciation of its significance.
3. Congratulate the recipient briefly and sincerely. Too flowery praise loses effectiveness.

Exercise 3

Try your hand at one of the letters just discussed. Follow the guides suggested for the letter you choose. Use correct letter form.

Postcard. A postcard is a miniature friendly letter. It is usually sent from a traveler to someone at home. The picture postcard often contains a photograph of some place the writer has visited. Because there is room for only a few sentences, the writer must be brief, yet also informative. A postcard can help cement friendships.

A postal card, which is sold by the post office with the stamp already imprinted, provides somewhat more space than a postcard. But it is also a letter in miniature. The postal card is often reserved for announcements of meetings, short news items, or hurried greetings. At times, it may serve as a substitute for a longer newsy letter.

How to Write a Travel Postcard

1. Write the date so that your friend will know when you wrote the card.
2. Avoid trite comments like ''Having a wonderful time. Wish you were here.''
3. Pick one or two interesting experiences on your trip and retell them briefly. Or describe one or two outstanding sights. Or tell about the photograph on a picture postcard.
4. Write your friend's name and address clearly.

Exercise 4: Studying a Sample Postcard

Study the following assignment to write a postcard. A sample postcard is included.

Directions: Write a postcard as instructed.

Situation: Choose either a trip you have actually taken or an imaginary trip based on something you saw on television or read.

Your task: Write a postcard with a message of three or four sentences to give your friend the flavor of the trip. Follow the preceding guides.

Sample Postcard

> July 12, 19—
>
> Dear Nelda,
> Florida's Sea World is all I hoped it would be. Baby Shamu, the whale born in captivity, imitates whatever its parents do. I got to pat a dolphin.
>   Love,
>   Doreen
>
> Ms. Nelda Torres
> 237 Arbor Street
> Southbury, CT 06488

Exercise 5: Writing a Travel Postcard

Using the directions for Exercise 4, write a travel postcard about an actual trip or about an imaginary one based on something you read or saw. Use the preceding sample as a guide.

Telephone Memos. A common responsibility today is the need to take a telephone message for someone else. The answering machine has assumed some of this responsibility, but in all probability you are sometimes called upon to take a message for a member of your family.

How to Take a Telephone Memo Accurately

1. Have near the telephone a pencil or pen and a pad on which to write the message. Avoid writing messages on shreds and scraps of paper.
2. Jot down the names of the person for whom the message is intended and the person who is making the call.
3. Note the time of the call and the date.
4. Write down the message briefly, accurately, and completely. Write legibly!
5. List the phone number of the person making the call.
6. Jot down your name.
7. Leave the memo in a conspicuous place, where it can be found.

Exercise 6: Studying a Telephone Memo

Now study a model telephone memo.

Directions: Write a telephone memo as instructed.

Situation: A friend has called a member of your family. Since the member is not home, you take down the message. The friend is calling to say that the time for the Camera Club meeting has been changed from Tuesday at 8:00 P.M. to Wednesday at 7:45 P.M. The caller asks that the family member bring to the meeting slides of the Quebec trip. The caller's telephone number is 555-7532.

Your task: Write the memo incorporating this information. In your memo, be sure to include all essential details as outlined in the guide.

Sample Telephone Memo

> *April 12, 19--, 7:00 P.M.*
>
> Sue
> Betty Wang called. Camera Club meeting postponed from this Tuesday at 8:00 P.M. to Wednesday at 7:45 P.M. Bring slides of Quebec trip. You can call her at 555-7532
>
> Jan

Exercise 7: Writing a Telephone Memo

Directions: Write a telephone memo as instructed.

Situation: A friend has called a member of your family to ask whether he or she can attend Saturday's football game. The caller has obtained the tickets.

Your task: Write the memo incorporating this information. In your memo, be sure to include all essential details as outlined in the guide. Use the sample as a model.

Exercise 8

Do you owe someone a letter? Check the following suggestions and write a letter that you could actually mail. Follow correct letter form. Review the suggestions listed throughout this section.

1. You have visited someone for lunch, overnight, or a few days. Or perhaps a friend has taken you along on a trip. Write the thank-you letter that expresses appreciation for the experience.
2. A friend in another city, or perhaps another country (a pen pal), has written to you. Answer the letter. Provide information that your friend will be interested in. Have your friend's letter at your side as you write.
3. You are planning a party or an exciting weekend. Invite a friend. Suggest some of the pleasant experiences you have decided upon.
4. A friend of yours has just won an honor—an athletic trophy, perhaps, or some scholastic award. Write a letter of congratulations.

12. Writing the Report

On a competency test, you may be expected to write a report. This assignment requires you to organize a number of bits of information into a forceful composition. You will be given full directions, but the organization will be left to you.

The report has all the characteristics of a good composition (page 43). Like the persuasive composition, it is generally expository in nature. It does not, however, require brainstorming.

If you prepare a report from scratch, these are the steps you must follow.

1. Decide what your audience is.
2. Choose a topic—neither too broad nor too narrow.
3. Examine various sources: encyclopedias, books, magazines, newspapers, television commentators, people you know.
4. Take notes, preferably on small library (3 × 5) cards. Also keep track of your sources.
5. Decide on important divisions of your report.
6. Shuffle the note cards around so that topics fall within their proper divisions.
7. Write a rough draft based on the shuffled note cards.
8. Revise and produce a finished product, suitable for the audience you have written for.

On a typical competency test, part of the work has already been done for you. The first four steps have been completed. You must take the task from there and work with steps 5–8.

How a Report Is Written

Let's study a report to see what must be done with the directions and notes supplied.

Directions: Write a report, using the situation and the set of notes below. Read *all* the information before you start to write.

Situation: Students in your social studies class have to prepare reports on scenic areas in the United States. You decided to write your report on Mt. Washington, in New Hampshire. You read several books and then interviewed your cousin, who has often hiked in the White Mountains. The notes you took during the interview and your reading are in the box on page 94. Numbers have been added to help you refer to each note individually.

1. Skiing in Tuckerman Ravine as late as June
2. Only Mt. Washington over 6,000 feet
3. Trails on eastern slope: Tuckerman Ravine, Lion's Head, Great Gulf
4. Trails on western slope: Crawford Path, Jewel
5. For visitors, a most popular peak in a popular range
6. Four of the highest peaks: Washington, Adams, Jefferson, Madison
7. Changeable, dangerous weather conditions
8. Great Gulf Trail unusually long and picturesque
9. Jewel Trail under Cog Railway to Summit House
10. White Mountains of New Hampshire ideal for hiking and climbing
11. Excellent for hikers in good condition
12. Old Crawford Path from Crawford Notch
13. Alpine Gardens on trails near summit
14. Presidential Range best of all
15. Across many peaks on Crawford Path
16. Alpine Gardens left from Ice Age

Your task: Organize these notes into a written report.

To help you organize and write your report, be sure to:

- Keep in mind that you are writing the report for your social studies class.

- Rearrange the notes before you start to write your first draft.

- Include *all* the information from the notes in your report.

There is the task. How should you begin? First, examine the notes carefully and begin to group those items together that seem to belong together.

Writing the First Paragraph

Number 10 seems like an excellent way to start off. It really gives you your first sentence, which is also your topic sentence:

The White Mountains of New Hampshire are ideal for hiking and climbing.

This sentence states the point of the report and suggests its direction. What else seems to belong in the opening paragraph?

Number 14 follows logically. The first sentence, on page 94, is a general statement. The second, below, is more specific.

Of these mountains, the Presidential Range is best of all.

Number 6, which identifies the peaks in the Presidential Range, follows.

Four of the highest peaks were named for the first four presidents: Washington, Adams, Jefferson, and Madison.

Number 2 adds a specific detail about one of the peaks, Mt. Washington. The next sentence in the paragraph takes this information and adds a little extra, which may be derived from all the notes.

Though only Mt. Washington is higher than 6,000 feet, all four peaks are impressive.

By grouping numbers 2, 6, 10, and 14, you have created your first paragraph, the introduction.

THE INTRODUCTION

> The White Mountains of New Hampshire are ideal for hiking and climbing. Of these mountains, the Presidential Range is best of all. Four of the highest peaks were named for the first four presidents: Washington, Adams, Jefferson, and Madison. Though only Mt. Washington is higher than 6,000 feet, all four peaks are impressive.

Note that you have created a good paragraph. It has a good opening topic sentence and a good closing, or clinching, sentence. It sticks to the topic. It uses connecting words and phrases like *of these mountains*, *four of the highest peaks*, and *though*.

You have taken care of paragraph 1. Where do you go from here? Though notes seem to fall naturally into certain groupings, different writers will see different combinations and ways of organizing the report. That's fine, as long as there is some logic to the arrangement. The organization that follows is one way of proceeding.

Writing Paragraph 2

Paragraph 1 has talked about hiking the Presidentials. Paragraph 2 seems to call for more information about hiking and the trails that are used. Number 11 seems to be a good opening sentence for paragraph 2.

> Hikers should be in good condition to attack Mt. Washington and the other peaks.

Why should hikers be in good condition? Number 7 tells us and suggests the second sentence of the paragraph.

> The weather is dangerous and can change at a moment's notice.

For your third sentence, you can combine numbers 1 and 3. The fact that there is skiing in June says something about the weather conditions, so this information can follow the sentence about the weather. But notice that number 3 also mentions Tuckerman Ravine. Here's an opportunity to combine two bits of information to make one solid sentence.

> The Tuckerman Ravine Trail brings skiers as late as June.

The fourth sentence uses the rest of the information from number 3.

> Other popular trails on the eastern slope include the Lion's Head Trail and the Great Gulf Trail.

Number 8 talks about the Great Gulf Trail. Use it to round out the paragraph.

> The Great Gulf Trail is unusually long and picturesque.

Now let's see what paragraph 2 looks like.

PARAGRAPH 2

> Hikers should be in good condition to attack Mt. Washington and the other peaks. The weather is dangerous and can change at a moment's notice. The Tuckerman Ravine Trail brings skiers as late as June. Other popular trails on the eastern slope include the Lion's Head Trail and the Great Gulf Trail. The Great Gulf Trail is unusually long and picturesque.

Writing Paragraph 3

You have grouped numbers 1, 3, 7, 8, and 11 to create a paragraph that follows paragraph 1 logically. Paragraph 2 is a complete unit in itself and is also part of a larger whole. Unity within a larger unity! Similarly, let's make paragraph 3 another complete unit of thought.

Since paragraph 2 talks about trails on the eastern slope, you might consider next those trails that cross the western slope. Since you'll be talking about western slope trails, you need a sentence to announce that fact. Create one.

Other trails approach from the western side.

Number 4 identifies two trails on the western slope, the Crawford Path and the Jewel Trail. Numbers 12 and 15 deal with the Crawford Path. Number 9 deals with the Jewel Trail. You have a choice here. Your next sentence can deal with either the Crawford Path or the Jewel Trail. Choose one.

The Jewel Trail winds its way to the Summit House underneath tracks of the Cog Railway.

Now that you've taken care of the Jewel Trail, you can go on to the Crawford Path. You can combine numbers 12 and 15 for the next sentence.

The old Crawford Path starts in Crawford Notch and crosses many peaks on its way to Mt. Washington.

You have not used two notes that deal with trails, numbers 13 and 16. This seems to be a good place for these notes. The next sentence develops the idea in number 13.

Many of these trails pass through lovely flowers near the summit.

The final sentence in the paragraph uses the idea in number 16.

These Alpine Gardens were left behind during the last Ice Age.

The third paragraph has now been completed (see page 98).

PARAGRAPH 3

> Other trails approach from the western side. The Jewel Trail winds it way to the Summit House underneath tracks of the Cog Railway. The old Crawford Path starts in Crawford Notch and crosses many peaks on its way to Mt. Washington. Many of these trails pass through lovely flowers near the summit. These Alpine Gardens were left behind during the last Ice Age.

Writing Paragraph 4

You now need a concluding paragraph. There is still one note left, number 5. How can you use this bit of information to create your final two sentences, your fourth paragraph?

THE CONCLUSION

> Mt. Washington is one of the most popular peaks in the United States. Any visitor to New Hampshire should try to include a visit to this rugged mountain and the entire Presidential Range.

Step by step, using the information provided in the notes, you have created a report that covers all the ground. It has used four paragraphs. The first paragraph introduces the subject. The fourth paragraph summarizes and closes it. Paragraphs 2 and 3 provide details to develop the topic.

Now let's see what the entire report looks like.

THE COMPLETE REPORT

> The White Mountains of New Hampshire are ideal for hiking and climbing. Of these mountains, the Presidential Range is best of all. Four of the highest peaks were named for the first four presidents: Washington, Adams, Jefferson, and Madison. Though only Mt. Washington is higher than 6,000 feet, all four peaks are impressive.
>
> Hikers should be in good condition to attack Mt. Washington and the other peaks. The weather is dangerous and can change at a moment's notice. The Tuckerman Ravine Trail brings skiers as late as June. Other popular trails on the eastern slope include the Lion's Head Trail and the Great Gulf Trail. The Great Gulf Trail is unusually long and picturesque.

> Other trails approach from the western side. The Jewel Trail winds its way to the Summit House underneath tracks of the Cog Railway. The old Crawford Path starts in Crawford Notch and crosses many peaks on its way to Mt. Washington. Many of these trails pass through lovely flowers near the summit. These Alpine Gardens were left behind during the last Ice Age.
>
> Mt. Washington is one of the most popular peaks in the United States. Any visitor to New Hampshire should try to include a visit to this rugged mountain and the entire Presidential Range.

What important characteristics does the report have?

1. It keeps a social studies emphasis, since it is being written for a social studies class.

2. It has rearranged the notes in a logical fashion and has presented a report that hangs together.

3. It has used *all* the information provided by the question.

4. It uses connecting words like *though*, *other*, *many*, and *these*.

5. It has a logical organization: introduction, eastern-slope trails, western-slope trails, conclusion.

Exercise 1: Preparing to Write a Report

Follow the directions below and prepare to write a report of the kind called for on a competency test. This first report will give you some extra help.

Directions: Write a report, using the situation and the set of notes given on page 100. Read *all* the information before you start to write.

Situation: Students in your English class have been asked to write a report on some community event. You decided to report on the Apple Festival, an annual week-long event. You have attended many of the events and have read about many of the others. The notes you took are in the box on page 100.

To help you in organizing this report, your first try, numbers have been added. Each number suggests the paragraph for which the note might be used.

4 Planning, a lot of work
3 Craft exhibitions: quilting, weaving, embroidery
2 Many entrants for competitions
3 Bluegrass band at folk dance
1 Apple Festival, an annual event
1 Community becomes one big family each September
2 Children's competitions: three-legged races, sack races
2 Adults' competitions: tennis, volleyball, softball
3 Displays of fruits, vegetables, canned goods
3 Folk-dance exhibition on Main Street
4 Planning takes months
4 Everyone grateful to committee after Festival
1 Something for everyone
1 All ages take part
1 Two major types: sports, exhibitions

Your task: Organize these notes into a written report. To help you organize and write your report, be sure to:

- Keep in mind that you are writing the report for your English class.

- Rearrange the notes before you start to write your first draft.

- Include in your report *all* the information from the notes.

Exercise 2: Writing a Report

Follow the directions below and prepare to write a report of the kind called for on a competency test. This time you will be completely on your own.

Directions: Write a report, using the situation and the set of notes given on page 101. Read *all* the information before you start to write.

Situation: Students in your health-education class have been asked to prepare reports on various contributions to good health. You decide to write a report on nutrition. You have consulted various reference books and have prepared the following notes.

Variety leading to better nutrition
Contents of average cereal box
Importance of fresh foods
Avoidance of too many processed foods
Sugar = ''empty calories''
Processed foods high in sugar
Eat balanced meals
Young people often careless about food
Follow rules for health and energy
Sugar keeps people from more important foods
Importance of vegetables
Young people often avoid cabbage, broccoli, carrots
Complex carbohydrates good: potatoes, whole grains
Good health depends on good nutrition
Careless young people may suffer when older
Shake the salt habit

Your task: Organize these notes into a written report. To help you organize and write your report, be sure to:

- Keep in mind that you are writing the report for your health-education class.

- Rearrange the notes before you start to write your first draft.

- Include *all* the information from the notes in your report.

13. Writing the Summary, or Précis

In recent years, frozen juice concentrates have played an ever more important part in meal planning. The concentrates make packaging and storing more convenient. Although a can of orange-juice concentrate is only about one-quarter of the original juice, it still contains the essential ingredients, with only water removed.

A **summary**, or **précis** as it is sometimes called, is like juice concentrate. It contains the essential ingredients of a reading passage, with only nonessential elements removed. Writing a summary combines reading skills and writing skills. Knowing how to write good summaries improves study, reading, note taking, and writing.

Condensing a message means eliminating everything but the essentials. Note how the second sentence below contains the essential elements of the first sentence but without the elaborating details.

Original Sentence: With much anticipation, our family visited Florida and camped in some of Florida's wonderful state parks, like Highlands Hammock, Gold Head Branch, and Hillsborough River.

Condensed: Our family camped in some of Florida's state parks.

The condensation is neither inferior nor superior to the original sentence. It has a different purpose: to present the gist of the message simply and directly. There are, of course, times when full details are called for. There are also times when it is necessary to cut to the bone to present a message or retain the heart of a message for future reference.

Practice: Summarizing

The brief reading passage below is followed by four possible summarizing sentences. Select the sentence that best summarizes the message of the selection.

> The popular game of checkers, often played as an easier substitute for chess, is deceptive. It is played on a simple-appearing checkerboard, but take heed. Because the rules seem simple and uncomplicated, some players get the mistaken idea that checkers is an easy game to learn, to play, and to master. Actually, nothing could be farther from the truth, for checkers is really trickier than it looks.

(a) Checkers and chess are both board games that are fun to play but not so easy to master.

(b) Because the rules of checkers are simple, players have the mistaken idea that checkers is an easy game to master.

(c) The checkerboard is a battleground on which a surprisingly complicated battle is waged between two players intent on winning.

(d) Checkers is not only a challenging game to play; it is also a challenge that attracts all who love puzzles.

Your answer: _____

Exercise 1: Writing a One-Sentence Summary

Using the practice exercise as a guide, write a one-sentence summary of the following reading passage. (A suggested summary appears at the end of this section, on page 108. You may wish to compare your version to it. Don't peek!)

> Once upon a time, coffeepots and teapots were very similar in appearance. There was no difference in their sizes and shapes. But over the years, their similarities disappeared, and they now tend to have quite different shapes, the teapot being wider and squatter.

Your summary: _____

_____

How to Write a Good Summary

1. Read the passage through to get the main idea. Write it down.
2. List the supporting points in order. Do not list minor details, quotations, repetitions, supporting examples, or figurative language.
3. Look up in the dictionary any unfamiliar words.
4. Write a rough draft. Use your own words as needed, but do not give your own ideas or opinions. Keep your eye on the passage. Use connecting words to make your ideas clear.
5. Make your summary about one-third or one-fourth the length of the original.
6. Write the final copy. Use correct English (pages 122–201).

Exercise 2: Studying How to Write a Summary

The following exercise shows how to write a summary from start to finish. First, read carefully the passage to be summarized.

The water hyacinth is a plant of the pickerelweed family native to tropical America. It has green leaves and spikes of violet flowers. The entire plant is actually quite pretty, but it is an undeniable nuisance. It was originally introduced into Florida as a decorative plant. The thoughtless action was soon regretted. The plant rapidly became a pest. The major difficulty was its habit of growth. It grew rapidly and seemed unstoppable. It choked rivers and other waterways. True, the rivers became beautiful carpets of green and violet, but the invader made navigation difficult.

A Florida engineer, E. Allen Stewart, was concerned about the destruction of Florida's environment. What could he do to help? He learned that the water hyacinth, though otherwise a pest, is actually a natural water purifier. Waste water treated by hyacinths is excellent. It is equal in quality to waste water treated by traditional purifiers, often superior. Stewart had a brilliant idea: to commercialize the purification process. His firm, called *Amasek*, sought and received purification contracts in Florida and elsewhere. The firm went a step further and even harvested the plants for animal food. Cows especially like to munch on chopped and dried water hyacinth plants. Stewart's experience shows that a dark cloud often does have a silver lining. His firm turned a disaster into a blessing and earned the thanks of all those interested in the environment.

How do you go about writing a summary? Begin by following these steps:

1. First, get the main idea.

    Though originally a pest, the water hyacinth now plays an important role in water-purification processes.

    You won't actually incorporate this main idea into your summary, but you will refer to it from time to time to check whether you are on the right track.

2. List the supporting points in order. What are they?

   A. The water hyacinth was introduced into Florida. It soon became a pest.

   Notice that this summarizes the first six sentences. Details like its family and place of origin have been omitted. That the plant is pretty is also a minor detail that has no place in a summary. When you learn that the hyacinth soon became a pest, you may reasonably assume that the action was regretted. You may thus eliminate sentence 5.

   B. The plant grew quickly. It choked rivers and other waterways.

   This summarizes the next three sentences.

   C. A Florida engineer learned that the hyacinth is a natural water purifier.

   This summarizes the next six sentences. The name of the engineer is an optional item to include, but it isn't essential. Other details have been excluded.

   D. His firm took on purification projects throughout Florida.

   This summarizes those sentences dealing with the commercial application of the hyacinth's special abilities.

   E. The firm even harvested the plants for animal food.

   This summarizes two sentences, combining the essential elements into one sentence. The mention of cows is a detail.

   F. The firm turned a disaster into a blessing.

   This condenses the last two sentences into one. It eliminates the figurative language about the dark cloud and the silver lining.

   Now it's time to write the summary itself. Just copying the preceding notes one after the other would result in a choppy paragraph. A certain amount of gracefulness is needed. This is how it's done.

A. After the water hyacinth was introduced into Florida, it soon became a pest.

This combines the first two sentences in the notes and adds a connective, *after*.

B. Because the plant grew quickly, it choked rivers and other waterways.

This also combines the two sentences and adds a connective, *because*.

C. Fortunately, a Florida engineer learned that the hyacinth is a natural water purifier.

This retains the note but adds a connective word, *fortunately*.

D. As a result, his firm took on purification contracts throughout Florida.

This retains the note but adds a connective, *as a result*.

E. The firm even harvested the plants for animal food.

F. It turned a disaster into a blessing.

E. and F. The firm even harvested the plants for animal food and turned a disaster into a blessing.

Since sentences in both E and F have the same subject (*the firm*), the new sentence combines both into a single sentence.

Now see how the summary looks when written in its complete form.

> After the water hyacinth was introduced into Florida, it soon became a pest. Because the plant grew quickly, it choked rivers and other waterways. Fortunately, a Florida engineer noticed that the hyacinth is a natural water purifier. As a result, his firm took on purification projects throughout Florida. The firm even harvested the plants for animal food and turned a disaster into a blessing.

How does this summary meet the characteristics of a good summary (page 103)?

1. The summary is entirely on the topic. It features the main idea throughout.
2. It eliminates minor details, supporting examples, and figurative language.
3. There were no unfamiliar words.
4. The summary does not include the writer's own ideas or opinions. It uses a number of connecting words to make the passage smoother and the ideas clearer.
5. It is between one-third and one-quarter the length of the original.
6. It uses correct English.

Exercise 3: Writing a Summary

Directions: Now try writing a summary of your own, using the preceding suggestions as a guide.

Situation: You have been presented with a reading passage, reproduced on page 108.

Your task: In your summary, be sure to:

- Read the passage carefully.
- Decide upon the main idea.
- Follow the how-to guide on page 103, eliminating all nonessentials.
- First, jot down the notes containing the basic information.
- Combine your notes in a rough draft to be used as the basis for the finished product.
- Write a smoothly flowing summary containing only essential information.

You have seen a great many attractive models on television and in magazines. Some of them you haven't really "seen." You've seen only their beautiful hands. Modeling is a highly competitive activity, but the specialized areas of hand modeling may be even more difficult to break into. Hand models are well paid—usually at least $250 an hour. One model, Trisha Webster, once earned $17,000 in a single week—just for having her hands photographed. Female beauty, so important in most modeling, is unimportant in hand modeling. There is a demand for both male and female models, though naturally the hands should be clearly recognizable as masculine or feminine.

Keeping hands perfect for camera work is a full-time job. Because cameras are pitiless, zooming in for closeups, hands must be free of faults—like poorly proportioned fingers—or blemishes—like warts or blotches. Surprisingly, the hands of a glamorous body model might be unsuitable for certain products. Indeed, there are "product hands" and "glamor hands," and they are usually quite different. Because so much is at stake, hands must be protected at all times. Hand models avoid the sun, wear gloves, and shun hard physical work of any kind. One model gave up playing the guitar. She had her cat declawed, opens taxi doors with knuckle and thumb, and opens pop-up cans with a spoon. A slight cut could put a hand model out of work for a week or more. As you might expect, there are other specialty models, as well as hand models. They are ready when a call goes out for ears, noses, lips, and other fragments of the human body.

Exercise 4

Write a summary of the passage on pages 71–72. Follow the guide on page 103.

Model Answer to Exercise 1, page 103

Once, coffeepots and teapots looked alike, but now they have characteristic shapes of their own.

14. Completing Forms

There is one kind of writing that is unavoidable. Throughout your life, you will have to fill out many forms. Here's a representative sample: job application, voter registration, absentee ballot, auto registration, driver's license, physician's health form, charge account, credit-card application, rebate request, Social Security, appliance warranty, marriage license, income-tax form, and application for a branch of the armed services.

"What's the problem?" you ask. "What's so hard about filling in some lines?" Surprisingly, forms are often filled out incorrectly. Wrong information, omissions, and misinterpretations are commonplace. Poorly filled out forms lose time, energy, money, and sometimes a job.

Can a person be trained to fill out forms accurately? The answer is *yes*. This section will help you anticipate many of the difficulties that are part of the process.

Gathering Information

All forms require basic information such as your name, address, and Social Security number. In addition, many forms ask for other personal information. If you are filling out an application in the personnel office of a business, for example, you should have needed information ready at hand. Fill in the following information now. If you aren't sure of certain information, look it up. Keep this form on file.

Here are some suggestions before you begin.

1. Read everything carefully.
2. Print neatly, in ink.
3. Be accurate and complete. Give area codes with telephone numbers and ZIP codes with addresses.

Exercise 1: Setting up a Personal Information File

DATE_____   SOCIAL SECURITY NUMBER_____

NAME

_____

Last   First   Middle initial

ADDRESS

_____

Street or post office box   City

_____

State and ZIP code   Phone number

PERSONAL INFORMATION

_____

Date of birth   Place of birth

_____

Height   Weight   Hair color   Eye color

_____

Father's name   Mother's maiden name

_____

Parent's address   Parent's telephone number

_____

In case of accident, notify . . .

_____

_____

Name, address, and telephone number of family physician

_____

_____

Name and address of bank in which you have an account

GENERAL HEALTH

_____

List any operations or injuries sustained.

_____

List any impairment in vision or hearing.

HOBBIES AND SPECIAL INTERESTS

_____

_____

SPORTS MOST ENJOYED

_____

_____

SCHOOL CLUBS OR OUTSIDE ORGANIZATIONS

_____

_____

EDUCATION (List all schools.)

_____

Elementary School   Location   Dates attended   Date of graduation

_____

High School   Location   Dates attended

EMPLOYMENT RECORD

_____

Name and address of employer   Dates of employment

_____

Name and address of employer   Dates of employment

VOLUNTEER WORK

_____

Project engaged in   Location and date

_____

Project engaged in   Location and date

SCHOOL REFERENCES (Teachers or administrators who might give you a good recommendation)

_____

Name   School   Location

_____

Name   School   Location

OTHER REFERENCES (Not a relative)

_____

Name   Address   How connected

_____

Name   Address   How connected

_____

Name   Address   How connected

As you grow older, additional information will be requested—for example, your marital status, the number of dependents, and your annual income. If you complete the form you have just worked on and keep it in a safe place, you'll be better prepared for most forms in your future.

Filling Out Sample Forms

Now that you have prepared your information file, you are ready to fill out some sample forms.

Application for a Credit Card

Most Americans enjoy the convenience of credit cards. Before a card can be issued, however, the applicant must provide some information about his or her financial condition. The form is really asking, "Are you a good credit risk?"

Exercise 2: Studying a Credit-Card Application Form

Though you are probably not ready to apply for a credit card now, you may be interested in seeing what kinds of information an application form asks you to provide. Study the application on page 113 and be ready to answer the questions below.

1. Why is the company interested in how long you have been living at your present address?

   _____

2. Why is the name of your employer important?

   _____

3. What is a co-borrower? Why must this person also supply information and sign the application?

   _____

4. Why does the form ask for your monthly salary and your financial worth (total assets)? Isn't this information too personal to divulge?

   _____

5. Why does the form insist that you list all your debts, or total obligations?

   _____

6. Many credit-card companies ask the card member to choose a rate for borrowing. A lower yearly fee requires a higher rate. A higher fee permits a lower rate. APR is the annual percentage rate on all debts not cleared up each month. Why is it advantageous to pay all obligations each month as they come

due? Why do so many people fail to do so, thus paying a fairly substantial rate of interest?

_____

_____

BORROWER INFORMATION	Personal Banker's Name	City Where I Bank		Checking Account No.	Other Accounts ☐ Checking ☐ Savings ☐ Loan
	Name			Birth Date / /	Social Security Number
	Address Street City State Zip			Years at This Address	Home Phone
	Previous Address Street City State Zip			How Long	Number of Dependents (excluding yourself)
	Employer			How Long	Business Phone
	Employer's Address Street City State Zip			Your Position	
	Previous Employer			How Long	Address
	Name of Nearest Relative Not Living With You	Relationship	Address		

NOTE: If this application is for a joint account, have the co-borrower fill out the co-borrower information below, and sign the bottom of the application where indicated.

CO-BORROWER INFORMATION	Name	Birth Date / /	Social Security Number
	Address same as above ☐ or:	Years at This Address	Home Phone
	Employer	How Long	Business Phone
	Employer's Address	Your Position	
	Previous Employer	How Long	Address
	Name of Nearest Relative Not Living With You Relationship Address		

NOTE: List all income, debts and references (attach separate sheet if necessary).

	MONTHLY SALARY	Alimony, child support or separate maintenance income need not be revealed if borrower or co-borrower does not wish it considered as a basis for repaying this obligation.	OTHER MONTHLY INCOME	$ Total
	Borrower Co-Borrower		Borrower Co-Borrower	

FINANCIAL INFORMATION	ASSETS (Description/In Name of)	$ Value	OBLIGATIONS (Company Name and City Location)	Account No.	$ Monthly Payment	$ Balance
	Real Estate		Rent/Mortgage			
	Autos		Autos			
	Boats/Rec. Vehicles		Line of Credit			
	Stocks/Bonds		Charge Accounts			
	Cash/Savings		Other			
	Other		Other			
	Other		Other			
	TOTAL ASSETS	$	TOTAL OBLIGATIONS		$	$

Has there ever been any Bankruptcy or Wage Earner proceeding filed by any party to this application?   ☐ Yes   ☐ No

Are there any unsatisfied liens or judgments against any party to this application?   ☐ Yes   ☐ no   (If explanation is necessary, attach additional sheet.)

Borrower _____   Co-Borrower _____

Voter Registration

If you are not yet a registered voter, you'll need to apply soon, since eighteen-year-olds are eligible to vote. Each state has its own voter registration form. The form on pages 114–115 is used in the state of New York for voter registration. New York, like many states, provides helpful instructions for filling out the form. Read the instructions as you are completing the form. The numbers at the left under "COMPLETION OF FORM" refer to the boxed numbers on the form.

Exercise 3: Filling Out a Voter Registration Form

FOLD HERE SECOND
Form 153-Rev. 1986

INSTRUCTIONS

COMPLETION OF FORM

1. Print your name and residence clearly. Do not give
2. post office box as residence. Include apartment, room
3. or floor number if part of address.

5. Print your mailing address if it is different from your residence address. Be sure to include the route or box number, if any.

8. Show in either years, months or days how long you have lived at this address. Circle time period which you are using.

11. If this is your first registration, write none in appropriate space. Otherwise print year and address from which last registered.

12. If answer to No. 12 is yes, continue to No. 13. If answer is no, provide information requested in section.

13. Enrollment in a political party is optional but you must be enrolled in a party in order to vote in a primary election of that party. Failure to check any box in this section will be considered as a desire not to be enrolled in a party.

13a. Check this box if you are already registered from your present address and are using this form to change your enrollment.

14. Sign and date within space provided. If you are unable to sign, your mark must be witnessed on the line indicated. Be sure to sign next to x on reverse side.

Be sure to include appropriate Board of Elections address on reverse side. It is a Class E felony for any applicant to procure a false registration or to furnish false information to the boards of election.

GENERAL INSTRUCTIONS

1. In order for your registration to be effective for the next general or special election, you must be a citizen of the United States, be 18 years old and a resident of the county, city or village for 30 days by the time of the election.

   Your application must be delivered to the board of elections not later than the 30th day before the election or postmarked not later than the 30th day and received by the board not later than the 25th day before the election in order to vote at that election.

2. Once you have registered you do not have to register again unless you move or fail to vote in a general, special or primary election for four consecutive years.

3. You will be notified by the board whether your application has been accepted or rejected. If you have not received this notice within 25 days after your application is submitted, you should contact the board.

4. In order for your registration and enrollment to be effective for the next primary election, your application must be filed with the board of elections not later than the 60th day before the primary election except that: (a) If you did not have the qualifications to vote at the last general election (age, citizenship, time at residence) you may apply up to 30 days before the primary election. (b) A transfer of enrollment (a registered voter moving within the State) must be filed at least 30 days before the primary election (c) If you change party enrollment, it will not be effective until after the next general election.

5. If additional assistance or information is required, contact your county board of elections.

FOLD UP ON PERFORATION FIRST   THIS WILL BE YOUR PERMANENT RECORD—PLEASE PRINT OR TYPE CLEARLY IN BLUE OR BLACK INK

FOR OFFICIAL USE ONLY

SERIAL NUMBER

Election District | Ward or A.D.

Date of Reg.

Cancellation

Date
Reason 1☐ 2☐ 3☐ 4☐ 5☐
6☐ 7☐ 8☐ 9☐ 10☐

Other Remarks

Democratic Registrar

Republican Registrar

1 Last Name | First Name | Initial | Jr. or Sr.

2 House Number | Street | Apartment Number

3 City or Town | 4 Zip Code | 6 Village (if any)

5 Mailing Address (if different)

7 Date of Birth | Sex | Height | Color of Eyes | 8 Length of Time at Residence | Yrs. or Mos. or Days | 9 Employer (Name & Address) | 10 Tel. No. (if listed)

11 Last Registered (Year) Number and Street (if none-state) | City or Town | County | State | Name by which Registered

12 Citizen by Birth? If No, Naturalization Papers | Yr. Issued City and State | Name by which Issued
☐Yes ☐No Complete ☐ Own ☐ Mother
(Following:) ☐ Spouse ☐ Father

13 **PARTY ENROLLMENT**

You must enroll in a party to vote in a primary. Check **ONE** box only in this section.

☐ Democratic ☐ Republican ☐ Conservative
☐ Liberal ☐ Right to Life ☐ I do not wish to enroll in party

13a ☐ This is a change of enrollment (See instruction 13a)

14 **AFFIDAVIT**

"I affirm that the information provided herein is true and I understand that this application will be accepted for all purposes as the equivalent of an affidavit, and if it contains a material false statement, shall subject me to the same penalties for perjury as if I had been duly sworn."

X

Signature or Mark of Applicant (sign within box) | Date

Witness to Mark (only if applicant is unable to sign) | Date
(MUST SIGN ON REVERSE SIDE)

DO NOT WRITE BELOW THIS LINE

Last Name | First Name | Initial | Jr.-Sr. | Street Address | City or Town | ED | Wd-AD

Application for Employment

One of the most important of all business forms is the job application. Personnel managers are impressed by neatness, completeness, and honesty. If you take the application form home, you may wish to type it. Keep in mind, however, that a neatly *printed* application is more impressive than a messy *typed* form. First impressions count for a great deal.

Exercise 4: Filling Out an Application for Employment

APPLICATION FOR EMPLOYMENT

PERSONAL INFORMATION

DATE _____   SOCIAL SECURITY NUMBER _____

NAME _____
     LAST   FIRST   MIDDLE

PRESENT ADDRESS _____
     STREET   CITY   STATE   ZIP CODE

PERMANENT ADDRESS _____
     STREET   CITY   STATE   ZIP CODE

PHONE NO. _____   OWN HOME _____   RENT _____   BOARD _____

DATE OF BIRTH _____   HEIGHT _____   WEIGHT _____   COLOR OF HAIR _____   COLOR OF EYES _____

MARRIED _____   SINGLE _____   WIDOWED _____   DIVORCED _____   SEPARATED _____

NUMBER OF CHILDREN _____   DEPENDENTS OTHER THAN WIFE OR CHILDREN _____   CITIZEN OF U. S. A.   YES ○   NO ○

IF RELATED TO ANYONE IN OUR EMPLOY, STATE NAME AND DEPARTMENT _____   REFERRED BY _____

EMPLOYMENT DESIRED

POSITION _____   DATE YOU CAN START _____   SALARY DESIRED _____

ARE YOU EMPLOYED NOW? _____   IF SO MAY WE INQUIRE OF YOUR PRESENT EMPLOYER? _____

EVER APPLIED TO THIS COMPANY BEFORE? _____   WHERE _____   WHEN _____

EDUCATION	NAME AND LOCATION OF SCHOOL	YEARS ATTENDED	DATE GRADUATED	SUBJECTS STUDIED
GRAMMAR SCHOOL				
HIGH SCHOOL				
COLLEGE				
TRADE, BUSINESS OR CORRESPONDENCE SCHOOL				

SUBJECTS OF SPECIAL STUDY OR RESEARCH WORK _____

WHAT FOREIGN LANGUAGES DO YOU SPEAK FLUENTLY? _____   READ _____   WRITE _____

U. S. MILITARY OR NAVAL SERVICE _____   RANK _____   PRESENT MEMBERSHIP IN NATIONAL GUARD OR RESERVES _____

ACTIVITIES OTHER THAN RELIGIOUS (CIVIC, ATHLETIC, FRATERNAL, ETC.) _____
EXCLUDE ORGANIZATIONS, THE NAME OR CHARACTER OF WHICH INDICATES THE RACE, CREED, COLOR OR NATIONAL ORIGIN OF ITS MEMBERS.

(Side margins: LAST / FIRST / MIDDLE)

(CONTINUED ON OTHER SIDE)

FORMER EMPLOYERS (LIST BELOW LAST FOUR EMPLOYERS, STARTING WITH LAST ONE FIRST.)

DATE MONTH AND YEAR	NAME AND ADDRESS OF EMPLOYER	SALARY	POSITION	REASON FOR LEAVING
FROM				
TO				
FROM				
TO				
FROM				
TO				
FROM				
TO				

REFERENCES: GIVE BELOW THE NAMES OF THREE PERSONS NOT RELATED TO YOU, WHOM YOU HAVE KNOWN AT LEAST ONE YEAR.

	NAME	ADDRESS	BUSINESS	YEARS KNOWN
1				
2				
3				

PHYSICAL RECORD:

LIST ANY PHYSICAL DEFECTS

WERE YOU EVER INJURED?   **GIVE DETAILS**

HAVE YOU ANY DEFECTS IN HEARING?   **IN VISION?**   **IN SPEECH?**

IN CASE OF EMERGENCY NOTIFY

NAME   ADDRESS   PHONE NO.

I AUTHORIZE INVESTIGATION OF ALL STATEMENTS CONTAINED IN THIS APPLICATION. I UNDERSTAND THAT MISREPRESENTATION OR OMISSION OF FACTS CALLED FOR IS CAUSE FOR DISMISSAL. FURTHER, I UNDERSTAND AND AGREE THAT MY EMPLOYMENT IS FOR NO DEFINITE PERIOD AND MAY, REGARDLESS OF THE DATE OF PAYMENT OF MY WAGES AND SALARY, BE TERMINATED AT ANY TIME WITHOUT ANY PREVIOUS NOTICE.

DATE   SIGNATURE

DO NOT WRITE BELOW THIS LINE

INTERVIEWED BY   DATE

REMARKS:

NEATNESS		CHARACTER	
PERSONALITY		ABILITY	

HIRED	FOR DEPT.	POSITION	WILL REPORT	SALARY WAGES

APPROVED: 1.   2.   3.

EMPLOYMENT MANAGER   DEPT. HEAD   GENERAL MANAGER

Change-of-Address Form

In these days of greater mobility, people are changing their residences more frequently than in the past. You must make sure that your mail is forwarded until your correspondents have your new address. For your convenience, the post office provides a handy form (see page 118). The front of the form is not shown.

Exercise 5: Completing a Change-of-Address Form

INSTRUCTIONS

INSTRUCTIONS: Complete Items 1 through 9 and the address on front of form. Please print, except for Item 8 which **requires your** signature.

1. Check only one block. If the entire family is moving from the old address, check entire family block. If a member of the family remains at the old address with the same last name, check individual move block and fill out a separate change of address order form for each person moving from the old household. If the move is for a business, check the block marked business.

2. Indicate the date which you want mail forwarding to begin.

3. If your move is **TEMPORARY** (you will be returning to your original household within twelve months) indicate the date to discontinue mail forwarding. If you fail to fill out this date, your mail will be treated as a permanent order and will continue to be forwarded.

4. Print **ONLY ONE** last name of person(s) moving to the same address. If person(s) with the same last name are moving from the same old address to different new addresses, use separate forms. If this is a business move, print name of business. If

more than one business is moving, separate forms must be completed.

5. If you have checked individual in Item 1, print first name of individual moving. If you have checked family move, print first name of the head of household, and include middle name or initials if they are commonly used. If business move, leave this item blank.

6. Print complete **OLD** address. If your **OLD** address is a rural route (RR), include the box number in the designated space. The abbreviation RR/HCR No. stands for Rural Route/ Highway Contract Route Number. If your **OLD** address includes an apartment number, please provide it.

7. Print complete **NEW** address. If your **NEW** address is a Rural Route, include the box number in the proper space. If your **NEW** address includes an apartment number, it is needed for accurate mail delivery.

8. This change of address order is not valid without your signature. See note on front of form.

9. Self-explanatory.
   COMPLETE ADDRESS PORTION ON FRONT OF FORM

Detach Before Mailing

U.S. Postal Service **CHANGE OF ADDRESS ORDER**	Customer Instructions: Complete Items 1 thru 9. Except Item 8, please PRINT all information including address on face of card.	**OFFICIAL USE ONLY**

1. Change of Address for *(Check one)* ☐ Individual ☐ Entire Family ☐ Business — Zone/Route ID No.

2. Start Date — Month Day Year | If TEMPORARY address, print 3. date to discontinue forwarding — Month Day Year | Date Entered on Form 3982 M M D D Y Y

4. Print Last Name or Name of Business *(If more than one, use separate Change of Address Order Form for each)* — Expiration Date M M D D Y Y

5. Print First Name of Head of Household *(include Jr., Sr., etc.)*. Leave blank if the Change of Address Order is for a business. — Clerk/Carrier Endorsement

6. Print **OLD** mailing address, number and street *(if Puerto Rico, include urbanization zone)*
Apt./Suite No.   P.O. Box No.   R.R/HCR No.   Rural Box/HCR Box No.
City   State   ZIP Code

7. Print **NEW** mailing address, number and street *(if Puerto Rico, include urbanization zone)*
Apt./Suite No.   P.O. Box No.   R.R/HCR No.   Rural Box/HCR Box No.
City   State   ZIP Code

8. Signature *(See conditions on reverse)*

9. Date Signed — Month Day Year

OFFICIAL USE ONLY — Verification Endorsement

OFFICIAL USE ONLY

PS Form 3575, Mar. 1988   ✿U.S.G.P.O. 1989 231-597

Application for a Driver's License

One form that nearly everyone must fill out at some time is the application for a driver's license. Application forms vary greatly from state to state. One of the most searching of all such forms is required by the state of Texas. After completing as much of the following application form as you can, you should be able to fill out the form for your own state.

Exercise 6: Completing an Application for a Driver's License

```
DL-14A (4/90)          APPLICATION FOR TEXAS              FOR DEPARTMENT USE ONLY
                                                          RESTRICTIONS/ENDORSEMENTS

  ☐ DRIVER'S LICENSE  A  B  C  M (Circle CLASS WANTED)
  ☐ INSTRUCTION PERMIT    ☐ COMMERCIAL DRIVER'S LICENSE
  ☐ IDENTIFICATION CARD   ☐ NON-COMMERCIAL DRIVER'S LICENSE
```

All information on this form except the signature must be TYPEWRITTEN or PRINTED in BLACK INK.
The signature shall be WRITTEN in BLACK INK.

Last Name	First Name	Middle Name	Maiden Name	Social Security Number

RESIDENCE ADDRESS   NUMBER AND STREET

		BIRTHDATE		
	MO.	DAY	YEAR	AGE NOW

CITY COUNTY	STATE OF DOMICILE	ZIP CODE	COLOR EYES	SEX	HEIGHT FT IN

MAILING ADDRESS (if different) STREET or BOX NO.	CITY	STATE	ZIP CODE	RACE	WEIGHT	NATURAL COLOR HAIR

PLACE OF BIRTH CITY	STATE

RESIDENT TELEPHONE NO.	PLACE OF EMPLOYMENT	BUSINESS TELEPHONE

➤ **INSTRUCTIONS:** If applying for **ID Card only** - answer Questions 1, 3 and 4 only.
If applying for a **Driver License** - answer all questions.

    NO YES   IDENTIFICATION CARD INFORMATION

1. ( ) ( ) Have you ever had a Texas Identification Card? Number _____ When? _____
                      DRIVING HISTORY
2. ( ) ( ) Are you enrolled or have you completed an approved driver education course?
3. ( ) ( ) Have you ever had a license or instruction permit in Texas?
            Number _____
4. ( ) ( ) Have you ever had a license or instruction permit in any other state?   Expired? Yes ___ No ___
            What State/s _____
            Number _____   Expired? Yes ___ No ___
5. ( ) ( ) Is your license or driving privilege now suspended, revoked, cancelled, denied or disqualified?
            Where? _____ When? _____ Why? _____
6. ( ) ( ) Has your license or driving privilege ever been suspended, revoked, cancelled, denied or disqualified?
            Where? _____ When? _____ Why? _____
7. ( ) ( ) Are you at this time placed out of service? Why? _____
                      FINANCIAL RESPONSIBILITY
8. ( ) ( ) Is the vehicle(s) you will use on the road test covered by an automobile liability insurance policy that meets the minimum re-
            quirements in Texas or exempt under the Act? (Exemptions: Government Vehicle; Certificate of Self-Insurance; Non-resident-
            Out of State Vehicle; Operated under Railroad Commission Permit.)
                      MEDICAL HISTORY
9. ( ) ( ) Do you have any physical defects such as ( ) missing limb, ( ) stiff neck, ( ) stiff arms or joints, ( ) loss of muscular con-
            trol, ( ) other _____?
10. ( ) ( ) Have you been under medication or hospitalized for a mental, nervous, or emotional condition within the past:
                ( ) one year if applying for Class C License?
                ( ) two years if applying for Class A or B License?
11. ( ) ( ) Have you had an epileptic seizure, convulsions, unexplained loss of consciousness, or other type of seizure within the past:
                ( ) one year if applying for Class C License?
                ( ) two years if applying for Class A or B License?
12. ( ) ( ) Do you have diabetes requiring treatment with insulin by injection?
13. ( ) ( ) Have you had a problem, been arrested, or hospitalized as a direct result of alcohol or drug abuse within the past:
                ( ) one year if applying for Class C License?
                ( ) two years if applying for Class A or B License?
14. ( ) ( ) Have you been diagnosed or hospitalized for ( ) dizziness, ( ) heart trouble, ( ) stroke, hemorrhage or clots,
                ( ) high blood pressure, ( ) blood vessel disorder, ( ) emphysema within the past:
                ( ) one year if applying for Class C License?
                ( ) two years if applying for Class A or B License?
15. ( ) ( ) Within the past two years, have you been treated for any other serious medical conditions? _____
16. ( ) ( ) Have you ever been referred to the Medical Advisory Board for Driver Licensing?
I DO SOLEMNLY SWEAR OR AFFIRM THAT I AM THE PERSON
NAMED AND DESCRIBED HEREIN AND THAT THE STATEMENTS
ON THIS APPLICATION ARE TRUE AND CORRECT   WRITE USUAL SIGNATURE _____

Department Use box (right side):

```
VISION TEST
          R       L      Both
        20/     20/     20/
UNCORRECTED

        20/     20/     20/
CORRECTED

COLOR        HEARING
Red    ☐     Deaf   ☐
Green  ☐     Poor   ☐
Normal ☐     Good   ☐

DRIVER EDUCATION
( ) Classroom
( ) Concurrent
( ) Laboratory
( ) M/C 20 Hour

ID PRESENTED
( ) Out of State
( ) Birth Cert.
( ) Passport
( ) _____
# _____

( ) O/S Attached
( ) O/S Lost
```

For Parent or Guardian if applicant is under age 18.
I do solemnly swear the above named applicant is my ( ) child ( ) stepchild
( ) ward; and that the information given on this application is true and correct. I authorize the Department of Public Safety to issue a Class ( ) A
( ) B ( ) C or ( ) M license to said minor.

False information could lead to charges being filed.
FINE: $2,000.00 and/or jail.
LEFT THUMB   RIGHT THUMB

_____
Signature of Parent or Guardian   Driver's License Number

Sworn to and subscribed before me this _____ day of
_____ 19 ___

_____
Notary Public or Authorized Officer

Application for a Social Security Card

By now you should have a Social Security card and number. If you must still apply for such a card, complete the blank form in Exercise 8 as preparation for making an application. If you already have a card, just answer the questions in Exercise 7.

Exercise 7: Studying a Social Security Application Form

After studying the application, answer these questions:

1. Must the applicant for the card be the person who fills out the form? Explain.

   _____

2. Which number in the form contains a request for information that may be disregarded?

   _____

3. Why is the mother's maiden name called for?

   _____

4. How does the form provide for a change in the applicant's name? (Note that marital status is not asked for.)

   _____

5. How does the form seek to correct any previous error?

   _____

Exercise 8: Filling Out a Social Security Application Form

SOCIAL SECURITY ADMINISTRATION
Application for a Social Security Card

Form Approved
OMB No. 0960-0066

INSTRUCTIONS
- Print or type using black or blue ink. DO NOT USE PENCIL.
- If you are completing this form for someone else, answer the questions as they apply to that person. Then, sign your name in question 16.

1 NAME
To Be Shown On Card ▶
FIRST   FULL MIDDLE NAME   LAST

FULL NAME AT BIRTH
IF OTHER THAN ABOVE   FIRST   FULL MIDDLE NAME   LAST

OTHER NAMES USED

2 MAILING ADDRESS
Do Not Abbreviate ▶
STREET ADDRESS, APT. NO., PO BOX, RURAL ROUTE NO.

CITY   STATE   ZIP CODE

3 CITIZENSHIP (Check One)
☐ U.S. Citizen ☐ Legal Alien Allowed To Work ☐ Legal Alien Not Allowed To Work ☐ Foreign Student Allowed Restricted Employment ☐ Conditionally Legalized Alien Allowed To Work ☐ Other (See Instructions On Page 2)

4 SEX ☐ Male ☐ Female

5 RACE/ETHNIC DESCRIPTION (Check One Only—Voluntary)
☐ Asian, Asian-American Or Pacific Islander ☐ Hispanic ☐ Black (Not Hispanic) ☐ North American Indian Or Alaskan Native ☐ White (Not Hispanic)

6 DATE OF BIRTH MONTH DAY YEAR

7 PLACE OF BIRTH (Do Not Abbreviate) CITY STATE OR FOREIGN COUNTRY FCI Office Use Only

8 MOTHER'S MAIDEN NAME FIRST FULL MIDDLE NAME LAST NAME AT HER BIRTH

9 FATHER'S NAME FIRST FULL MIDDLE NAME LAST

10 Has the person in item 1 ever received a Social Security number before?
☐ Yes (If "yes", answer questions 11-13.) ☐ No (If "no", go on to question 14.) ☐ Don't Know (If "don't know", go on to question 14.)

11 Enter the Social Security number previously assigned to the person listed in item 1.

☐☐☐ – ☐☐ – ☐☐☐☐

12 Enter the name shown on the most recent Social Security card issued for the person listed in item 1.

FIRST MIDDLE LAST

13 Enter any different date of birth if used on an earlier application for a card. MONTH DAY YEAR

14 TODAY'S DATE ▶ MONTH DAY YEAR **15 DAYTIME PHONE NUMBER** ▶ ( ) AREA CODE

DELIBERATELY FURNISHING (OR CAUSING TO BE FURNISHED) FALSE INFORMATION ON THIS APPLICATION IS A CRIME PUNISHABLE BY FINE OR IMPRISONMENT, OR BOTH.

16 YOUR SIGNATURE ▶

17 YOUR RELATIONSHIP TO THE PERSON IN ITEM 1 IS:
☐ Self ☐ Natural Or Adoptive Parent ☐ Legal Guardian ☐ Other (Specify)

DO NOT WRITE BELOW THIS LINE (FOR SSA USE ONLY)

NPN		DOC	NTI	CAN		ITV
PBC	EVI	EVA	EVC	PRA	NWR	DNR	UNIT

EVIDENCE SUBMITTED

SIGNATURE AND TITLE OF EMPLOYEE(S) REVIEWING EVIDENCE AND/OR CONDUCTING INTERVIEW

DATE

DCL DATE

PART II

Review of Common Usage Problems

In the writing part of many competency tests, you may be asked to write a letter, a report, or some other form of composition. Your writing should be reasonably free of usage errors, including errors of spelling, punctuation, and capitalization. This section of the book provides a quick but inclusive review of usage rules that you should already know but may have forgotten. By refreshing your memory about problems of usage, you will be more likely to write letters, reports, and compositions with confidence—and competence.

1. Problems with Sentence Structure

There are three basic kinds of sentences. The names of them are less important than your ability to write them correctly. However, knowing their names makes it possible to discuss them clearly.

Simple Sentences

In school, you have learned that a sentence must have a **subject** and a **verb.** The verb is often called a **predicate.** In the following sentences, the subject has one line under it; the verb has two.

Maria sang.

A section of the bridge fell during the recent storm.

The above are *simple sentences.* Each one contains a subject and a verb. Either the subject or the verb, or both, may be *compound.* Something that is compound has two or more parts.

Simple Sentences with Compound Parts

Compound subject: <u>Maria</u> and <u>Jeffrey</u> sang.

Compound verb: Maria <u>sang</u> and <u>danced</u>.

Compound subject and verb: <u>Maria</u> and <u>Jeffrey</u> <u>sang</u> and <u>danced</u>.

Practice 1: Creating Simple Sentences with Compound Parts

Each numbered line consists of two sentences. You are to combine each pair into one simple sentence with compound parts. The finished sentence may have either a compound subject or a compound verb. (You will have to make some minor changes.)

1. Mario plays tennis. Carla also plays tennis.

_____

_____

2. The boat caught fire. It finally sank.

_____

_____

3. We visited Washington, D.C. We toured the city.

_____

_____

4. Helen bought some roses. She put them in a vase on the table.

_____

_____

5. The Tigers play their games in our stadium. The Lions, too, play their games in our stadium.

_____

_____

Compound Sentences

Two or more simple sentences can be combined to form a *compound sentence.*

Simple sentence: Dogs show affection for their masters.

Simple sentence: Cats are more aloof.

Compound sentence: Dogs show affection for their masters, but cats are more aloof.

The parts of a compound sentence are often joined together by **and, but, or,** or **nor.** These "joining words" are called *coordinating conjunctions.*

When two sentences are joined to make a compound sentence, the two main parts are called *clauses.* Because these two parts can stand by themselves as complete sentences, they are called *independent clauses.*

Compound sentence: The bells rang, AND students quickly filled the corridors.

Compound sentence: Are you coming to the game, OR have you made other plans?

Compound sentence: Helen doesn't like lima beans, NOR does she care for okra. (To identify subject and verb, arrange the sentence in subject-verb order: "she does care for okra.")

Practice 2: Creating Compound Sentences

Combine each pair of sentences to form a good compound sentence. Use **and, but, or,** or **nor.** Make slight changes in wording, if necessary.

1. You may think of Dobermans as vicious dogs. Many of them are gentle.

_____

_____

2. Babies require care and attention. They become sickly.

_____

_____

3. Lightning struck the tree. The bark peeled off in layers.

_____

_____

4. Jim did not mow the lawn. He did not trim the rosebushes.

_____

_____

5. The rain poured down. The sun was shining.

_____

_____

Complex Sentences

A **complex sentence** has two or more clauses, too, but at least one of the clauses cannot stand by itself as a sentence. Note the following example.

Complex sentence: If Paula calls, give her my message.

First clause: If Paula calls, (*subordinate clause*)

Second clause: give her my message. (*independent clause*)

The *first clause* cannot stand by itself as a sentence. Although it has both a subject and a verb, it needs something to complete its thought. It is a **subordinate clause.** The *second clause* can stand by itself. It is an **independent clause** with the understood subject *you*.

Subordinate Clauses

Many students have difficulty with subordinate clauses in their writing. They sometimes make the mistake of punctuating subordinate clauses as if they were complete sentences.

Subordinate clauses begin with connectives, or "joining words," called **subordinating conjunctions.** Here's a partial list.

after	before	than	until
although	how	though	when
as	if	till	while
because	since	unless	why

In the following sentences, the conjunctions are capitalized; the subordinate clauses are circled; and the independent clauses are underlined.

Complex sentence: Juan went home WHEN the game ended.

Complex sentence: BEFORE the movie started, Eleanor bought popcorn.

Practice 3: Finding Subordinate Clauses

Circle the subordinate clause in each sentence. Draw a line under each clause that could stand by itself as a sentence.

1. After the newscast ended, I began my homework.

2. I won't leave until Cindy arrives.

3. The rain will get heavier before it stops.

4. Although Martha loves ice cream, she is going on a diet.

5. When the snapshots are ready, get them from the camera store.

More on Subordinate Clauses

Another type of subordinate clause begins with the pronoun **who, which,** or **that.** In the following sentences, the subordinate clauses are circled. As you see, they cannot stand by themselves as sentences.

Complex sentence: Ellen is the girl (WHO won the golf match.)

Complex sentence: Brooklyn, (WHICH is now part of New York City,) was once a separate city.

Complex sentence: The part of the movie (THAT I liked best) was the ending.

Practice 4: Subordinate Clauses with WHO, WHICH, and THAT

Circle the subordinate clause in each sentence. Be careful not to circle a part of the independent clause.

1. Georgia Bonesteel, who teaches a course in lap quilting, is a friend of Nancy's.

2. The Statue of Liberty is the sight that greeted millions of new immigrants.

3. Basketball, which was invented by an American, is now played around the world.

4. Itzhak Perlman is a man who has overcome serious physical disabilities.

5. One plant that everyone should avoid is poison ivy.

Exercise 1: Identifying the Three Basic Kinds of Sentences

Identify each sentence by writing SIMPLE, COMPOUND, or COMPLEX on the line.

1. The movie was very interesting, but I enjoyed the book more.

    1. _____

2. Her flight was canceled, and the trip was postponed.

    2. _____

3. Alton Cramer, who was chosen to represent our school, could not attend the meeting.

    3. _____

4. The teachers and the students stood together.

    4. _____

5. The car skidded and almost struck a utility pole.

    5. _____

6. Lisa replaced the record that she had broken.

    6. _____

7. Are you planning a new wardrobe?

    7. _____

8. She used her personal computer to do her longer homework assignments.

    8. _____

9. When buses are delayed, students are usually late for school.

    9. _____

10. Disneyland and Hollywood are popular places to visit in California.

    10. _____

Exercise 2: Writing Complex Sentences

Combine each pair of sentences to make one strong complex sentence. If you need help, look again at the list of subordinating conjunctions on page 125.

1. The sunrise was beautiful. A storm rolled in by eleven.

    _____

    _____

2. Roger came home early. Marjorie was late.

    _____

    _____

3. Tom plays professional football. His brother is more skilled in baseball.

    _____

    _____

4. My brothers Rodney and Sid are going skiing. The snow is deep enough.

   _____

   _____

5. I wrote to the senator. She never received my letter.

   _____

   _____

6. I will have to wait a long time to buy my concert ticket. The lines of people are blocks long.

   _____

   _____

7. Jeff is on the track team. He finished next to last in the first race.

   _____

   _____

8. Don't forget to water the flowers. They require more moisture at this time of year.

   _____

   _____

9. The lawyer rose slowly. The jury looked at him with expectation.

   _____

   _____

10. Angelo was studying in his room. Noisy construction was going on outside.

    _____

    _____

Sentence Fragments

It is important to be able to write complete sentences. Competency tests check for your ability to do this. When a group of words does not express a complete thought, it is a *sentence fragment.* Here are some examples of sentence fragments. Although they begin with a capital letter and contain end punctuation, they are not complete sentences. Study the ways that they can be made into complete sentences.

No verb: Alice, along with a friend of hers from Dallas.

Complete sentence: Alice arrived, along with a friend of hers from Dallas.

No verb: A small puppy running unsteadily across the lawn. (The word *running* by itself is not a verb. It needs a helping verb like *is* or *was*. See pages 135, 152, and 153.)

Complete sentence: A small puppy was running unsteadily across the lawn.

No subject: Took the train from Boston to New Haven.

Complete sentence: He took the train from Boston to New Haven.

No verb, no subject: From my uncle in Dallas.

Complete sentence: I got a gift from my uncle in Dallas.

A common error is using a prepositional phrase as a complete sentence. A **preposition** shows the relation of the noun or pronoun following it to some other word in the sentence. A **phrase** is a group of connected words that do not contain a subject or a predicate.

Prepositional phrase: Near the telephone on the table.

Complete sentence: A lamp stood near the telephone on the table.

Practice 5: Making Fragments into Complete Sentences

Rewrite each sentence fragment as a complete sentence. Add words as needed.

1. At the bus stop on the corner near the K-Mart store.

   _____

   _____

2. Phil, unhappy with the test results.

   _____

   _____

3. Lost my new wristwatch somewhere in the locker room.

   _____

   _____

4. Enjoying the cool breezes of the Pocono Mountains.

   _____

   _____

5. A rerun of *Star Wars* playing at the local theater.

   _____

   _____

6. A television set in one corner and a videocassette recorder nearby.

   _____

   _____

7. Carried the groceries from the car to the kitchen.

   _____

   _____

8. The football team lining up for the kickoff.

   _____

   _____

9. Winning the game at the final whistle.

   _____

   _____

10. The lead singer with the band behind him on the stage.

    _____

    _____

Exercise 3: Writing Complete Sentences

Rewrite each sentence fragment as a complete sentence. Add whatever words are necessary.

1. Because I had never tasted eggplant before.

   _____

   _____

2. A lost library book lying on a bench in the locker room.

   _____

   _____

3. A heavy freeze, a cause of many accidents on the slick roads.

   _____

   _____

4. Solved the third math problem after half an hour of hard work.

   _____

   _____

5. Along the bank of the Columbia River.

_____

_____

6. At the dog show, puppies and dogs of every size and breed.

_____

_____

7. Driving to the rehearsal of *Charley's Aunt,* the school play.

_____

_____

8. Our best pitcher finding himself in trouble in the sixth inning.

_____

_____

9. Walked the mile in a comfortable 20 minutes.

_____

_____

10. The autumn trees in a patchwork of yellows, reds, and purples.

_____

_____

Subordinate Clauses as Fragments

Subordinate clauses are not complete sentences.

Subordinate clause: Unless you are here by six o'clock.

Complete sentence: Unless you are here by six o'clock, I will have to leave.

Subordinate clause: When suddenly the traffic on Main Street came to a halt.

Complete sentence: We were driving home when suddenly the traffic on Main Street came to a halt.

Subordinate clause: Which is a major Egyptian industry.

Complete sentence: Much money comes into the country from tourism, which is a major Egyptian industry.

A sentence fragment that consists of a subordinate clause can be corrected in two ways. One way is by eliminating the subordinating conjunction. The other way is by adding words to complete the thought.

Subordinate clause: When Julia won.

Complete sentence: Julia won. (The subordinating conjunction *when* is eliminated.)

Complete sentence: I was happy when Julia won. (Words are added to complete the thought.)

Practice 6: Correcting Sentence Fragments

Make each fragment into a complete sentence. In any five of the sentences, eliminate the subordinating conjunction. In the other five, add words to complete the thought.

1. Although I had never seen Joan before.

   _____

   _____

2. Unless Charles changes his mind.

   _____

   _____

3. Why the refrigerator made a loud noise.

   _____

   _____

4. After we had packed a picnic lunch.

   _____

   _____

5. Until the coach decides on a starting pitcher.

   _____

   _____

6. If a blizzard hits the city tonight.

   _____

   _____

7. Since you are a good friend of Nelda's.

   _____

   _____

8. When we won the first four games.

   _____

   _____

9. Since we arrived at the concert on time.

   _____

   _____

10. As storm clouds threatened.

    _____

    _____

Exercise 4

Make each fragment into a complete sentence. In any five of the sentences, eliminate the subordinating conjunction. In the other five, add words to complete the thought.

1. When the clock struck twelve.

   _____

   _____

2. Because I live at a great distance from school.

   _____

   _____

3. How I found my lost ring.

   _____

   _____

4. Since I had never taken craft work before.

   _____

   _____

5. As the snow slowly sifted down through the trees.

   _____

   _____

6. Until Ted came with the key to the exercise room.

   _____

   _____

7. Whenever the dogs saw a squirrel.

   _____

   _____

8. Before we arrived at the picnic.

   _____

   _____

9. Although Jerry doesn't usually like chocolate.

   _____

   _____

10. While Marcy was calling home.

    _____

    _____

Verbals as Fragments

Most of us play more than one role in life. You may be both a student and an athlete. Your father may be a gardener and a bank officer. Your sister may be a singer and an actress. All three of you have different functions in each role. Playing two or more roles is a part of life.

Some kinds of words also play two roles. A **verbal** is such a word. The suffix *al* means *like*; a verbal is *like a verb*, but is not a verb. As the name suggests, it has a verb role, but it also acts as another part of speech. There are three different kinds of verbals: participles, gerunds, and infinitives. (See pages 33–34.)

Participles

A participle acts as both a verb and an adjective.

> We found Dot *painting* a decoy.
> (*Painting* modifies *Dot*, like an adjective, and takes an object, *decoy*, like a verb.)

> *Exhausted* by the heat, we all jumped into the cool mountain stream.
> (*Exhausted* modifies *we*, like an adjective, and in turn is modified by a prepositional phrase, *by the heat*, like a verb.)

> *Having pitched* a perfect game, Jerry spoke to the reporters.
> (*Having pitched* modifies *Jerry*, like an adjective, and takes an object, *game*, like a verb.)

A participle cannot make a complete sentence without a true verb.

Not a sentence: Donna jumping up and down with a hornet sting.

Sentence: Donna was jumping up and down with a hornet sting.
  (The helping verb *was* completes the verb.)

Sentence: Donna jumped up and down with a hornet sting.

Not a sentence: Lenore packing a lunch for the picnic.

Sentence: Lenore packed a lunch for the picnic.

Sentence: Packing a lunch for the picnic, Lenore used Swiss cheese, pickles, and ham.

For avoiding dangling modifiers, see pages 21–22.

Gerunds

A gerund acts as both a verb and a noun.

> I enjoy *riding* my bike in the early morning.
> (*Riding* is the object of *enjoy*, like a noun. It takes an object, *bike*, like a verb.)

> *Driving* a car in a crowded modern city requires concentration and good nerves.
> (*Driving* is the subject of *requires*, like a noun. It takes an object, *car*, like a verb.)

A gerund cannot make a complete sentence without a true verb.

Not a sentence: Winning the soccer match with a penalty kick.

     Sentence: Winning the soccer match with a penalty kick delighted the fans from Argentina.

     Sentence: Argentina won the soccer match with a penalty kick.

Infinitives

An infinitive can act as a noun, an adjective, or an adverb. An infinitive usually appears with *to*.

> Jeremy tried *to add* a Nero coin to his collection of Roman coins.
> (*To add* is the object of *tried*, like a noun. It takes an object, *coin*, like a verb.)

> The first person *to solve* the puzzle wins.
> (*To solve* modifies *person*, like an adjective. It has a direct object, *puzzle*, like a verb.)

> We used dry kindling *to start* the campfire.
> (*To start* modifies *used*, like an adverb. It takes an object, *campfire*, like a verb.)

An infinitive cannot make a complete sentence without a true verb.

Not a sentence: To gather blackberries for a pie.

     Sentence: We decided to gather blackberries for a pie.

     Sentence: We gathered blackberries for a pie.

Practice 7

Each of the following uses a verbal in place of a verb. Rewrite each to make a complete sentence. Use the suggestions in the preceding pages.

1. Our dog racing madly through the house in pursuit of our cat.

   _____

   _____

2. To cut down a dead pine near the house.

   _____

   _____

3. Finding a four-leaf clover in the meadow near home.

_____

_____

4. Hoping for an answer to her letter.

_____

_____

5. An electrician to repair the short circuit in the wall socket.

_____

_____

Exercise 5

Each of the following uses a verbal in place of a verb. Rewrite each to make a complete sentence. Use the suggestions in the preceding pages.

1. To visit Rocky Mountain National Park this summer.

_____

_____

2. Dad frying pancakes in a smoky kitchen.

_____

_____

3. Having wrapped the package securely.

_____

_____

4. To warm up on a really cold winter's day.

_____

_____

5. Eating a well-balanced meal.

_____

_____

6. A good plan to win at checkers.

_____

_____

7. To see a Gilbert and Sullivan operetta for the first time.

_____

_____

8. Lying down on a soft bed of pine needles.

_____

_____

9. Seeing a blind person on the corner of a busy intersection.

_____

_____

10. To apply for a part-time job in a fast-food restaurant.

_____

_____

Run-on Sentences

Writing sentence fragments is a serious error. Writing run-on sentences is an equally serious error. A _run-on sentence_ is two or more sentences written as if they were one sentence.

Run-on sentence:	I enjoy puzzles they keep me entertained on rainy days.
Separate sentences: (_correct_)	I enjoy puzzles. They keep me entertained on rainy days.
Run-on sentence:	There was a loud splash, Fido had jumped into the pond.
Separate sentences: (_correct_)	There was a loud splash. Fido had jumped into the pond.

Practice 8: Correcting Run-on Sentences

Rewrite the following run-ons. Make them into two separate sentences.

1. That cabinet is beautiful, it adds to the decor of the room.

_____

_____

2. Teresa enjoys swimming her brother Tom prefers boating and fishing.

_____

_____

3. Are you ready to leave do you have the tickets?

   _____

   _____

4. I dislike the laugh track on television comedies, the laughs sound so false.

   _____

   _____

5. The business of renting videotapes is booming there are two new rental stores in town.

   _____

   _____

Change Run-ons to Compound and Complex Sentences

Some run-on sentences can be corrected by adding an appropriate connecting word.

Run-on sentence:	Video games require good coordination, players must react quickly.
Compound sentence: (*correct*)	Video games require good coordination, and players must react quickly.
Run-on sentence:	Phyllis goes to evening school, she wants to become an X-ray technician.
Complex sentence: (*correct*)	Phyllis goes to evening school because she wants to become an X-ray technician.

The following words can lead to run-on sentences: *also, hence, nevertheless, then, therefore,* and *thus.* These words are not conjunctions. They cannot join sentences with only a comma. Sometimes a semicolon is used.

Run-on sentence:	The driver stopped, then he got out of his car.
Separate sentences: (*correct*)	The driver stopped. Then he got out of his car.
Run-on sentence:	My best subject is science, therefore I took a science elective this year.
With semicolon: (*correct*)	My best subject is science; therefore, I took a science elective this year.

Practice 9

Change the following run-ons into compound or complex sentences.

1. The Jets are a winning team, they have a good defense.

   _____

   _____

2. Maryanne practiced ballet for two hours, she is in a special performance.

   _____

   _____

3. The light was shining in my eyes, I pulled the shade down.

   _____

   _____

4. George entered the supermarket, he went to the bakery section.

   _____

   _____

5. Julie was driving too fast, she slowed down very soon.

   _____

   _____

6. I opened the door the phone rang.

   _____

   _____

7. Rosita got a good grade on the test, she studied very hard.

   _____

   _____

8. Mr. Carson doesn't jog every day, he doesn't swim anymore.

   _____

   _____

9. Shake the bottle of medicine, take two drops in water.

   _____

   _____

10. She listened to the radio, she had earphones on.

    _____

    _____

Exercise 6

Get rid of all sentence fragments. Correct the run-on sentences. Add or eliminate words as needed.

1. If she were elected president of the Spanish Club.

   _____

   _____

2. Have you ever seen the locks on the St. Lawrence Seaway, they are fascinating.

   _____

   _____

3. With a cry of triumph at the end of the long, hard tennis match.

   _____

   _____

4. Visited my grandmother in Greenville.

   _____

   _____

5. The dog barked noisily, then a car pulled into the driveway.

   _____

   _____

6. Why don't you plan a visit to the American Museum of Natural History, it has a superb collection of gems.

   _____

   _____

7. When bats fluttered low over our campsite.

   _____

   _____

8. Four runners standing on the starting line.

   _____

   _____

9. Which had been closed for repairs.

   _____

   _____

10. The boys' team won four of their matches the girls' team won five of theirs.

_____

_____

Exercise 7: Writing the Three Basic Kinds of Sentences

Follow the directions carefully to create the sentences below.

1. Write a simple sentence with a compound subject.

_____

2. Write a compound sentence.

_____

3. Write a complex sentence.

_____

4. Write a complex sentence with a subordinate clause beginning with _that_.

_____

5. Write a simple sentence with a compound subject and a compound verb.

_____

6. Write a compound sentence using _or_.

_____

7. Write a simple sentence with a compound verb.

_____

8. Write a complex sentence with two subordinate clauses.

_____

_____

9. Write a sentence with a subordinate clause beginning with _if_.

_____

10. Write a complex sentence with two independent clauses.

_____

_____

2. Problems with Nouns

There are two main problems with nouns. The first is forming *plurals*. The second is forming *possessives*. When you have to form plural possessives, you are faced with both problems.

Plurals of Nouns

1. **To form the plurals of most nouns, add s.**

apple—apple**s**	friend—friend**s**
desk—desk**s**	shoe—shoe**s**
train—train**s**	message—message**s**

2. **To form the plurals of nouns ending in s, ch, sh, x, or z, add es.** (This gives the word an extra syllable and makes it easier to pronounce.)

address—address**es**	tax—tax**es**
church—church**es**	waltz—waltz**es**
dish—dish**es**	lunch—lunch**es**

3. **To form the plurals of nouns ending in y preceded by a CONSONANT, change y to i and add es.**

ally—all**ies**	lady—lad**ies**
company—compan**ies**	navy—nav**ies**
country—countr**ies**	secretary—secretar**ies**
cry—cr**ies**	ferry—ferr**ies**

   The vowels are **a, e, i, o**, and **u**. The consonants are all the other letters of the alphabet. The letter *y* acts as a vowel in words like *myth* and a consonant in words like *yes*.

   Nouns ending in y preceded by a VOWEL add only s.

alley—alley**s**	ray—ray**s**
valley—valley**s**	holiday—holiday**s**
alloy—alloy**s**	attorney—attorney**s**

4. **To form the plurals of some nouns ending in f or fe, add s.**

belief—belief**s**	handkerchief—handkerchief**s**
fife—fife**s**	roof—roof**s**
gulf—gulf**s**	safe—safe**s**
chief—chief**s**	proof—proof**s**

5. To form the plurals of other nouns ending in **f** or **fe**, change the **f** to **v** and add **es**.

calf—cal**ves**   knife—kni**ves**
leaf—lea**ves**   life—li**ves**
shelf—shel**ves**   loaf—loa**ves**
wife—wi**ves**   self—sel**ves**

Nouns ending in **ff** always add **s**.

cliff—cliff**s**   cuff—cuff**s**

Practice 1: Writing Plurals

Write the plural form of each of the following nouns.

1. baby _____   9. pony _____
2. bunch _____   10. stone _____
3. crash _____   11. story _____
4. puff _____   12. tank _____
5. glass _____   13. tray _____
6. half _____   14. key _____
7. miss _____   15. wax _____
8. pinch _____

6. To form the plurals of most nouns ending in **o**, add **s**.

alto—alto**s**   piano—piano**s**
dynamo—dynamo**s**   rodeo—rodeo**s**
Eskimo—Eskimo**s**   soprano—soprano**s**

These familiar nouns ending in **o** have plural forms with **es**.

echo—echo**es**   tomato—tomato**es**
hero—hero**es**   veto—veto**es**
potato—potato**es**   torpedo—torpedo**es**

7. To form the plurals of most compound nouns, add **s**.

classroom—classroom**s**   cupful—cupful**s**
schoolbook—schoolbook**s**   teaspoonful—teaspoonful**s**

8. A few nouns form their plurals in special ways, without adding s or es.

child—children   mouse—mice
deer—deer   ox—oxen
foot—feet   series—series
goose—geese   tooth—teeth
man—men   woman—women

Practice 2

Write the plural form of each of the following nouns.

1. mouthful _____   6. piano _____

2. echo   _____   7. roof _____

3. foot   _____   8. hero _____

4. textbook _____   9. potato _____

5. sheep   _____   10. tooth _____

Exercise 1: Writing Plurals

Write the plurals of these nouns.

1. strawberry _____   6. saleswoman _____

2. chef   _____   7. branch   _____

3. government _____   8. attorney   _____

4. bookshelf _____   9. family   _____

5. radio   _____   10. foot   _____

Possessives of Nouns

To show possession, use the *possessive* form: the *boy's* bicycle. The possessive singular is easy to form. The possessive plural takes some thought.

9. To form the possessive of a singular noun, add apostrophe s ('s).

cat + 's   ⟶   cat**'s**
woman + 's   ⟶   woman**'s**
son-in-law + 's   ⟶   son-in-law**'s**

Practice 3: Writing Singular Possessives

Write the singular possessive form of each of the following nouns.

1. animal   _____   7. igloo _____
2. attorney-general   _____   8. sister _____
3. brother   _____   9. nurse _____
4. commander in chief   _____   10. week _____
5. fox   _____   11. man _____
6. girl   _____   12. year _____

10. **To form the plural possessive of any noun, take the following two steps,** *one at a time.*

FIRST: Write the plural. (Don't omit this step!)
Notice the last letter in the plural form.

If plural ends in s: *If plural does not end in s:*

artist—artist**s**   child—childre**n**
astronaut—astronaut**s**   man—me**n**
rocket—rocket**s**   sheep—shee**p**
trainer—trainer**s**   woman—wome**n**

SECOND: (*a*) If the plural form ends in **s**, add an apostrophe (').
           (*b*) If the plural form does not end in **s**, add an apostrophe and an **s** ('**s**).

If plural ends in s,   *If plural does not end in s,*
add an apostrophe.   *add an apostrophe and an s.*

artist**s'** easels   children**'s** games
astronaut**s'** training   men**'s** jackets
rocket**s'** red glare   sheep**'s** clothing
trainer**s'** advice   women**'s** movement

That's all there is to it. If you follow the two steps, you will never go wrong.

Practice 4: Writing Plural Possessives

Write the plural possessive form of each of the following nouns. *Remember:* First write the plural. Then add an ' or '**s** as needed.

1. athlete _____   4. four-year-old _____
2. city _____   5. goose _____
3. salesman _____   6. house _____

7. mouse _____   10. search _____

8. month _____   11. tree _____

9. parent _____   12. wolf _____

Exercise 2: Writing Possessives

Write the singular possessive, plural, and plural possessive of each of the following nouns.

Singular	Singular Possessive	Plural	Plural Possessive
1. book			
2. man			
3. box			
4. lady			
5. sheep			
6. brush			
7. rose			
8. punch			
9. calf			
10. safe			
11. friend			
12. cage			
13. pie			
14. infielder			
15. ox			
16. mouse			
17. nurse			
18. deer			
19. carpenter			
20. judge			
21. hero			
22. athlete			
23. story			
24. monkey			
25. chief			

Exercise 3: Writing Plurals and Possessives

Write the correct form of the noun in parentheses as required by the sense of the sentence.

1. He left two of his (*book*) _____ on the bus.

2. The (*book*) _____ cover was torn.

3. Bill drove his (*sister*) _____ car.

4. The two (*sister*) _____ bought two (*house*) _____ .

5. The hunter shot three (*goose*) _____ .

6. The ranger found that many of the (*goose*) _____ wings were broken.

7. Two of Mr. Dixon's (*daughter*) _____ own a computer store.

8. The two (*daughter*) _____ store is on Main Street.

9. Both of my (*brother*) _____ belong to the (*school*) _____ bowling team.

10. Ten of the hotel's (*doorman*) _____ worked on Sunday.

3. Problems with Verbs

Every sentence has one or more verbs. When you construct sentences, you have to pay close attention to the verbs. You must choose the correct tense of the verb. You must also make the verb agree with its subject. The following review will refresh your memory about the use of verbs.

Using the Correct Tense

Tense means "time." The form of a verb shows the time of the action that the verb expresses. Be sure to use the correct tense in your writing.

Present tense: A statue of Thomas Jefferson *stands* in Washington, D.C.

Past tense: The old Brooklyn Dodgers *played* at Ebbets Field.

Future tense: Shirley *will meet* the bus at 5:00 this afternoon.

Present perfect tense: The Pyramids *have lasted* for thousands of years.

Past perfect tense: By late afternoon, all the guests *had left*.

Future perfect tense: By the year 2000, people's taste in popular music *will have changed*.

Keeping to the Same Tense

A common mistake is to mix the present and the past in a sentence. Stick to the same tense. Study the two examples to see how to correct errors.

Mixed tenses: I <u>lose</u> my keys and <u>waited</u> for my mother to come home.
         present   *past*

Same tense: I <u>lose</u> my keys and <u>wait</u> for my mother to come home.
        present   *present*

Same tense: I <u>lost</u> my keys and <u>waited</u> for my mother to come home.
        past   *past*

Mixed tenses: Because she <u>misses</u> the bus, she <u>walked</u> to school.
            present   *past*

Same tense: Because she <u>misses</u> the bus, she <u>walks</u> to school.
          present   *present*

Same tense: Because she <u>missed</u> the bus, she <u>walked</u> to school.
          past   *past*

Practice 1: Keeping to the Same Tense

The following sentences show inconsistent use of tense, mixing present and past. Make each pair of verbs consistent.

In 1–3, make all verbs present tense.

1. I get up at 7:00 A.M. and took a quick shower.

_____

_____

2. Children splashed in the neighborhood pool while the lifeguards supervise carefully.

_____

_____

3. The puppies played at Mother's feet as she knits quietly in the rocker.

_____

_____

In 4–6, make all verbs past tense.

4. The school bus was late, but I get an excuse note from the driver.

_____

_____

5. We hike up the Mt. Greylock trail and rested on the summit.

_____

_____

6. I asked our football coach to put me on the team, but he says I am too late.

_____

_____

Exercise 1: Keeping to the Same Tense

The following sentences show inconsistent use of tense, mixing present and past. Make each pair of verbs consistent.

In 1–3, make all verbs present tense.

1. Helen strolls into the school cafeteria and sat down next to Hal Cook.

_____

_____

2. Alex walked bravely to the front of the room and addresses the class.

   _____

   _____

3. Dad handed the tiller to me and then ducks as the boom swings over.

   _____

   _____

In 4–6, make all verbs past tense.

4. Ben thinks for a moment and then explained his point of view.

   _____

5. The 727 circled Greenville Airport and then heads toward Atlanta.

   _____

   _____

6. The players slip up behind Bill Parcells and dumped a bucket of Gatorade on him.

   _____

   _____

Principal Parts of Verbs

Regular Verbs

Most verbs are *regular*. They form tenses (express time of an action) in regular, predictable ways.

> I **wash** the dishes.
> (Expresses an action taking place, or an action always true.)

> I **washed** the dishes.
> (Expresses an action gone by.)

> I **have washed** the dishes.
> (Expresses an action completed at the time of speaking.)

Irregular Verbs

Some verbs are *irregular*. They cause trouble because they do not form their tenses in the usual way.

> I **see** a UFO.   I **saw** a UFO.
> (Expresses an action taking place.)   (Expresses an action gone by.)

> I **have seen** a UFO.
> (Expresses an action completed at the time of speaking.)

Principal Parts of Irregular Verbs

A speaker or writer of correct English must know the principal parts of irregular verbs. For example,

We don't say: We swimmed to the float.
We DO say: We **swam** to the float.

We don't say: Dad has went to the office.
We DO say: Dad **has gone** to the office. (*Has* is a helping verb.)

We don't say: The girls have ate their lunch.
We DO say: The girls **have eaten** their lunch. (*Have* is a helping verb.)

Here is a list of the trickiest irregular verbs. Study them thoroughly.

PRINCIPAL PARTS OF 40 IRREGULAR VERBS

Present	*Past*	*Past Participle*
am	was	(have) been
become	became	(have) become
begin	began	(have) begun
blow	blew	(have) blown
break	broke	(have) broken
bring	brought	(have) brought
catch	caught	(have) caught
choose	chose	(have) chosen
come	came	(have) come
do	did	(have) done
draw	drew	(have) drawn
drink	drank	(have) drunk
drive	drove	(have) driven
eat	ate	(have) eaten
fall	fell	(have) fallen
find	found	(have) found
freeze	froze	(have) frozen
get	got	(have) gotten *or* got
give	gave	(have) given
go	went	(have) gone
hold	held	(have) held
know	knew	(have) known
leave	left	(have) left
lie	lay	(have) lain
ride	rode	(have) ridden
rise	rose	(have) risen
say	said	(have) said
see	saw	(have) seen

shake	shook	(have) shaken
sit	sat	(have) sat
speak	spoke	(have) spoken
stick	stuck	(have) stuck
swim	swam	(have) swum
take	took	(have) taken
teach	taught	(have) taught
tear	tore	(have) torn
throw	threw	(have) thrown
win	won	(have) won
wind	wound	(have) wound
write	wrote	(have) written

Forms of *have*, like forms of *be* and *do*, are often used as helping verbs: *has left, were chosen, do agree.*

Practice 2: Choosing the Correct Principal Part of the Verb

In each sentence, underline the correct form of the verb.

1. At the fair, we (**saw, seen**) a tractor-pulling contest.
2. The Coopers (**brought, brung**) the hot dogs to the picnic.
3. Phyllis has (**chose, chosen**) dramatics as her English elective.
4. Mr. Esposito (**did, done**) a good job in landscaping his yard.
5. You missed Vera. She has (**gone, went**) to the movies.
6. I have never (**ate, eaten**) a more delicious dish than stuffed flounder.
7. Oh, I've (**tore, torn**) my jacket.
8. Melanie has (**drawn, drew**) a picture of our cabin in the Catskills.
9. I (**been, have been**) taking tennis lessons this summer.
10. The old maple tree in the forest has (**fallen, fell**) at last.
11. Bud (**came, come**) late to the Camera Club meeting.
12. That old hat has (**laid, lain**) on the desk for a week.
13. Yesterday's storm has (**shaken, shook**) most of the apples from the tree.
14. Raul (**swam, swum**) forty laps in the pool yesterday.
15. Have you (**gave, given**) old clothes to the Dramatics Club?
16. As we entered town, the village clock (**began, begun**) to strike.
17. During our move to Phoenix, three of our lamps were (**broke, broken**).
18. Paolo thought he (**knew, knowed**) the girl who had just entered the store.
19. Has any quarterback ever (**throwed, thrown**) a football 70 yards?
20. The weather at the soccer game turned cold, and we were nearly (**froze, frozen**).
21. ''Lazy Days'' is the best composition Doreen has ever (**written, wrote**).
22. Have you ever (**ridden, rode**) on a Pasofino horse?

23. The noon whistle (**blew, blowed**) ten minutes late today.

24. Have you ever (**spoke, spoken**) before a full auditorium?

25. Sue has never (**driven, drove**) a car at night.

Exercise 2: Choosing the Correct Principal Part of the Verb

In each sentence, underline the correct form of the verb.

1. I (**been, have been**) the team mascot for two years.

2. The quarterback (**saw, seen**) a receiver uncovered and completed the pass.

3. This year, Jack Brown (**became, become**) the first pitcher to win ten games.

4. The leaves are (**laying, lying**) in the driveway ankle deep.

5. Suellen (**catched, caught**) a five-pound bass in the lake.

6. I was so thirsty I (**drank, drunk**) a whole quart of lemonade.

7. Get up! The sun has already (**risen, rose**).

8. Esther and Dot have (**taken, took**) the sandwiches.

9. Mrs. Adams has (**taught, teached**) for 30 years.

10. Until yesterday, Dad had never (**driven, drove**) a sports car.

11. Peg Revman (**did, done**) a good job with that craft work.

12. Doug Palmer (**brought, brung**) an old Perry Como record to the luncheon.

13. Essie has (**broke, broken**) all club records for lowest golf score.

14. Abe has (**spoke, spoken**) to Fred about the condition of the tennis courts.

15. June Murtha has (**chose, chosen**) her courses for next semester.

16. John Elway (**threw, throwed**) the ball 65 yards in the air for a touchdown.

17. Nathaniel (**drawed, drew**) a picture of a dinosaur to accompany his story.

18. Have you ever (**ridden, rode**) in a Landrover over bumpy roads?

19. Jonathan has (**swam, swum**) to the float in the middle of the lake.

20. By the time we remembered the apples on the porch, they had (**froze, frozen**).

21. The wind has (**blowed, blown**) hard all night long.

22. Ann (**knew, knowed**) that Ted would arrive on time.

23. Marie (**began, begun**) to have doubts about arriving on time in Memphis.

24. Oh, I've (**tore, torn**) my new trousers!

25. I had never (**ate, eaten**) chick peas before yesterday.

Agreement of Subject and Verb

A verb must agree with its subject in *number*. That is, if the subject of a sentence is singular, the verb must also be singular: "The *child is* lost." If the subject is plural, the verb must also be plural: "Your *friends are* here."

	Singular	*Plural*
First person:	I enjoy	we enjoy
Second person:	you enjoy	you enjoy
Third person:	he, she, it enjoys	they enjoy

The verb *to be*, the commonest verb in English, is, alas, irregular. These are the present-tense forms:

	Singular	*Plural*
First person:	I am	we are
Second person:	you are	you are
Third person:	he, she, it is	they are

These are the past-tense forms:

I was	we were
you were	you were
he, she, it was	they were

The important verb *to have* is worth a look. These are the present-tense forms:

First person:	I have	we have
Second person:	you have	you have
Third person:	he, she, it has	they have

These are the past-tense forms:

I had	we had
you had	you had
he, she, it had	they had

Most native speakers of English tend to use the right form in sentences, like the one below, in which the verb follows the subject.

A <u>tree</u> <u>stands</u> at the front gate.

In other sentences, subject-verb agreement, not as simple as the above, is the cause of some common mistakes. So study these few rules.

1. **A difficulty comes when there are words** (those in parentheses below) **between the subject and the verb.**

A <u>tree</u> (with green leaves) <u>stands</u> at the front gate.

Some people would mistakenly write *stand* in the belief that *leaves* is the subject. It is not.

2. Expressions like *together with*, *according to*, *including*, *as well as*, and others do not affect subject-verb agreement.

> The <u>players</u>, including the coach, <u>are going</u> to the game by plane.

In the above sentence, *players* is the subject, not *coach*.

3. Another common difficulty arises in agreement when the subject is compound. The words *and*, *or*, *nor*, *either . . . or*, *neither . . . nor* signal the presence of a compound subject.

a. When two subjects are connected by *and*, the subject is plural and the verb is usually plural.

> High <u>seas</u> AND dense <u>fog</u> <u>have slowed</u> the rescue operation.

b. When two singular subjects are joined by *or* or *nor*, the subject is singular and the verb is singular.

> <u>Rain</u> OR <u>snow</u> <u>is</u> the forecast for today.

c. When two subjects of different number are joined by *neither . . . nor* or *either . . . or*, the verb agrees with the nearer subject.

> NEITHER <u>Fran</u> NOR her <u>brothers</u> <u>are going</u> to the state convention.

> EITHER these telephone <u>numbers</u> OR that <u>address</u> <u>is</u> wrong.

4. *You* always takes a plural verb. "You was" is wrong.

> <u>You</u> <u>were listed</u> on today's honor roll.

> <u>Were</u> <u>you</u> <u>expecting</u> the honor?

5. When the subject comes after the verb, find the subject and make the verb agree with it.

> (**Was, Were**) the nominees for Best Actor all present at the Academy Awards ceremony?
> (The subject is *nominees*. Therefore, *were* is correct.)

There (**was, were**) three raccoons digging in the rubbish heap.
(The subject is *raccoons*, not the introductory word *there*. *Were*
is correct. *Here* is a similar introductory word.)

In a corner of my desk (**are, is**) the schedules for the Spurs'
basketball games and the Bears' football games.
(The subject is *schedules*. *Are* is correct.)

Practice 3: Making Verbs Agree with Their Subjects

In each sentence, underline the correct form of the verb.

1. The books on that shelf (**are, is**) biographies.
2. The coach, together with his players, (**are, is**) having pictures taken.
3. The elm and the chestnut (**is, are**) subject to a deadly disease.
4. Neither the president nor the other officers (**was, were**) present at the lecture.
5. A good food for dogs (**contain, contains**) the right balance of vitamins and minerals.
6. Either the Denby Brothers or Wu Chen (**are, is**) my choice for first place in the competition.
7. The windows as well as the door (**was, were**) locked.
8. A woman representing local consumer organizations (**speak, speaks**) tonight in the auditorium.
9. The two lamps on my father's desk (**are, is**) old but still in working order.
10. A hamburger or a frank (**are, is**) not enough for my lunch.
11. I was happy when you (**was, were**) chosen class president.
12. There (**was, were**) several garnets in that rock you found.
13. On top of the mountain (**are, is**) two huge boulders, easily seen from below.
14. Here (**come, comes**) the clowns!
15. (**Was, Were**) you surprised to find your watch in that old jacket?

Exercise 3: Making Verbs Agree with Their Subjects

In each sentence, underline the correct form of the verb.

1. Mary Jane (**doesn't, don't**) know whether or not to wear the ghost costume to the party.
2. The front tires of that old Dodge (**are, is**) worn and smooth.
3. The first clock to strike the hours (**was, were**) constructed in 1754 by Benjamin Banneker.
4. Aunt Ginny, with her two daughters, (**are, is**) arriving on the ten o'clock train from Danville.
5. Fog, with poor visibility, (**are, is**) often a problem on the coast.
6. There (**was, were**) several good scoring opportunities in the playoff game between the Pirates and the Reds.

7. At the masquerade, (**was, were**) you the vampire with the long cloak?

8. At the intersection of Church Street and Main (**are, is**) two beautiful maple trees.

9. Four moons of Jupiter (**are, is**) visible with good binoculars.

10. Heavy rainfall during September and October (**help, helps**) to keep down forest fires.

11. One of the twins (**are, is**) taking Russian next semester.

12. Neither the coach nor his assistants (**was, were**) available for an interview after the game.

13. Either broccoli or asparagus (**are, is**) suitable for tonight's dinner.

14. In the barn (**was, were**) two ancient tractors still in good running order.

15. (**Was, Were**) there any doughnuts left from the meeting?

Troublesome Verb Pairs

Some verb pairs seem to cause more than their share of difficulty. Learn to use correctly each verb in the following pairs.

Lie, Lay

First, study the forms of these tricky verbs.

Present	Present Participle	Past	Past Participle
lie (''rest,'' ''recline'')	lying	lay	lain
lay (''put'' or ''set down'')	laying	laid	laid

Notice these correct forms:

Angela is *lying* down. She *lay* down an hour ago. She has *lain* on the couch without stirring.

Mr. Winters is *laying* the tile. He *laid* most of the tile yesterday. He has *laid* tile for a number of builders.

Sit, Set

Present	Present Participle	Past	Past Participle
sit (''occupy a chair'')	sitting	sat	sat
set (''place,'' ''put in order'')	setting	set	set

Notice these correct forms:

> Nathan is *sitting* on the front porch. He *sat* in his favorite rocker. He has *sat* in that chair many times.

> The twins are *setting* the table. They *set* it this morning, too. They have *set* it every day this week.

Learn, Teach

To learn is to gain knowledge. *To teach* is to give knowledge. Notice these correct forms:

> When Miss Trapani *teaches* science, I *learn* more easily.

Bring, Take

To bring usually calls for motion toward the speaker. *To take* usually calls for motion away from the speaker. Notice these correct forms:

> When you come home from school today, please *bring* me an evening newspaper.

> Please *take* this overdue book to the library.

Adapt, Adopt

To adapt means to change, to adjust. *To adopt* means to take as one's own. Notice these correct forms:

> Animals like the opossum learn to *adapt* to new climates and living conditions.

> Our dog Sabrina has *adopted* the kitten Doug brought home.

Practice 4: Using Troublesome Verbs Correctly

In each sentence, underline the correct form in parentheses.

1. Wake up Dad. He has (**laid, lain**) in that hammock all afternoon.
2. At my brother's graduation, our family was (**setting, sitting**) in the third row of the auditorium.
3. Nobody can (**teach, learn**) you anything if you resist instruction.
4. Please (**bring, take**) this saw down to the workbench in the basement.
5. A species that cannot (**adapt, adopt**) to changing conditions is doomed to extinction.

Exercise 4

On line (b), rewrite sentence (a) by changing the agreement of the subject and verb. If the subject is singular, make it plural. If plural, make it singular. The first one is done for you.

1. (a) Joanne walks to the library.
   (b) Joanne and Bill walk to the library.

2. (a) Two rosebushes grow by the door.
   (b) _____

3. (a) The child plays ball.
   (b) _____

4. (a) The whistle blows at noon.
   (b) _____

5. (a) The bill is overdue.
   (b) _____

Exercise 5: Using Troublesome Verbs Correctly

In each sentence, underline the correct form of the verb.

1. Our cat Tigger has been (**laying, lying**) in that chair all afternoon.
2. My father (**learned, taught**) me to drive.
3. All four paws and the tail of the black kitten (**was, were**) black.
4. Our puppy Tagalong (**adapted, adopted**) us, not the other way around.
5. Please (**bring, take**) this fresh squash to Mrs. Hancock.
6. It (**doesn't, don't**) matter if you can't finish the book by Friday.
7. The barn, with the surrounding buildings, (**was, were**) threatened by the brush fire.
8. Granddad is (**setting, sitting**) on the front porch, watching the world go by.
9. When (**was, were**) you finally able to finish your term paper?
10. Either the encyclopedia or the unabridged dictionary (**are, is**) likely to have an illustration of a lift pump.
11. There (**are, is**) many excellent recipes for spaghetti.
12. It was a lazy day, and we (**laid, lay**) on the beach most of the morning.
13. Please (**learn, teach**) me how to use the word processor.
14. Travelers must (**adapt, adopt**) their ways to those of the country visited.
15. An Abyssinian cat and a Himalayan cat (**are, is**) pictured on a single United States stamp.

4. Problems with Modifiers

Nouns and verbs carry the essential thought of a sentence. These are the bread-and-butter words, the key content words, the power words. Other kinds of words, called *modifiers,* add exactness and color to sentences. Notice the difference they make.

> 1. Monkeys chattered.
> 2. A hundred monkeys chattered noisily.

The bare sentence in 1 is considerably enriched by the added modifiers in sentence 2.

An *adjective* modifies (tells something about) a noun. An *adverb* modifies (tells something about) a verb. In sentence 2 above, *hundred*, an adjective, modifies the noun *monkeys*. *Noisily*, an adverb, modifies the verb *chattered*.

Adjectives and Adverbs Confused

A common problem with modifiers is to confuse adjectives with adverbs. The usual error is to use an adjective when an adverb is needed.

1. Pierce did *well* on his science test. (NOT *good*)

2. Jerry sometimes speaks too *rapidly*. (NOT *rapid*)

3. Young birds in nests must be fed *regularly*. (NOT *regular*)

4. Meg looked *thoughtfully* at her test paper before beginning to write. (NOT *thoughtful*)

5. To teach any animal tricks, you must work *patiently* with it. (NOT *patient*)

Practice 1: Choosing the Correct Modifier

In each sentence, underline the correct modifier in parentheses.

1. You cannot do (**good, well**) if you don't have enough sleep.
2. The runaway truck careened (**wild, wildly**) down the road before running into a ditch.
3. After only two lessons, Mary plays golf very (**good, well**).
4. The river current was rushing too (**swift, swiftly**) for safe swimming.
5. Our relay team ran (**good, well**), but we still came in second.

Double Negatives

A *negative* is a "no" word such as *no, not, never, nobody, nothing, hardly,* or *scarcely.* The *n't* in a contraction (as in *don't*) is a negative. A ***double negative*** occurs when TWO negatives are mistakenly used to make one negative statement. The remedy? Simply remove one of the negatives.

The examples below show two ways of removing one of the negative words.

Negatives

TWO: I do<u>n't</u> have <u>no</u> homework tonight.
ONE: I have <u>no</u> homework tonight.
ONE: I do<u>n't</u> have any homework tonight.

TWO: Joan is<u>n't</u> going to have <u>nothing</u> to do with you.
ONE: Joan is going to have <u>nothing</u> to do with you.
ONE: Joan is<u>n't</u> going to have anything to do with you.

TWO: Do<u>n't</u> <u>never</u> read the final pages of a detective story first.
ONE: <u>Never</u> read the final pages of a detective story first.
ONE: Do<u>n't</u> ever read the final pages of a detective story first.

TWO: There are<u>n't</u> <u>hardly</u> any sandwiches left.
ONE: There are <u>hardly</u> any sandwiches left.
ONE: There are almost <u>no</u> sandwiches left.

TWO: <u>Nobody</u> is<u>n't</u> left to play quarterback.
ONE: <u>Nobody</u> is left to play quarterback.
ONE: There is<u>n't</u> anybody left to play quarterback.

Practice 2: Avoiding Double Negatives

In each sentence, underline the correct word in parentheses.

1. That haircut makes Brian look as if he hasn't (**any, no**) hair.
2. There isn't (**any, no**) more lemonade in the jug.
3. Pauline doesn't go (**anywhere, nowhere**) without her pocket calculator.
4. The light was so dim I (**could, couldn't**) hardly read the message.
5. Don't (**ever, never**) cross the street against the light.

Other Common Errors

1. Don't add *s* to *anyway, anywhere, everywhere, nowhere, somewhere.*

My Spanish book must be somewhere$ around here.

2. **Don't say** *this here* **or** *that there* **to describe a noun.**

   This ~~here~~ cake was made without eggs.

3. **Don't use** *more* **with an** *-er* **word (***more wiser***) or** *most* **with an** *-est* **word (***most prettiest***).**

   Our cat is ~~more~~ smarter than our cocker spaniel.

4. **Don't use** *them* **as the subject of a verb.**

   Those
   ~~Them~~ are the best pancakes I've ever eaten.

Practice 3: Avoiding Some Common Errors

In each sentence, underline the correct form in parentheses.

1. (**That, That there**) innocent-looking plant is poison ivy.
2. We searched all morning, but our beagle was (**nowhere, nowheres**) to be found.
3. The (**most newest, newest**) show on television is a science-fiction special.
4. (**Them, Those**) are the peaches I bought at the supermarket.

Exercise: Choosing the Correct Modifier

In each sentence, underline the correct modifier in parentheses.

1. Don't answer too (**rapid, rapidly**).
2. The gymnast performed her routine (**careful, carefully**).
3. The car (**isn't, is**) hardly moving.
4. Fred doesn't have (**any, no**) work to do tonight.
5. (**Anyway, Anyways**), he never works on Tuesdays.
6. The old man was (**more wiser, wiser**) than his grandson.
7. (**Them, Those**) boats are unsafe in deep water.
8. (**This here, This**) bike is better than that one.
9. Which do you think is the (**more, most**) expensive of the two cars?
10. (**Nowheres, Nowhere**) in the parking lot was there an empty space.

5. Problems with Pronouns

Personal Pronouns

Subjects and Objects

A handful of pronouns cause more trouble than all the rest put together. These *personal pronouns*, as they are called, have different forms when used as subjects and as objects. Here are the troublemakers:

	Singular			*Plural*	
As subjects:	I	he	she	we	they
As objects:	me	him	her	us	them

Notice that these pronouns are paired. Your choice in a sentence would be between *I* and *me*, for example. *I* is the form used for the subject and *me* for the object.

> *I* watched the Bears game Monday night.
> (*I* is the subject of the verb *watched*.)

> Helen told *me* about the surprise party for Luis.
> (*Me* is the object of the verb *told*.)

Most pronoun difficulties occur when two pronouns are joined by *and*. When in doubt, say what you would say if each pronoun stood alone.

> Laura and *she* (not *her*) competed in the spelling bee.
> (*She* is one-half of the compound SUBJECT of the verb *competed*.)

> Check yourself. Say:
>   Laura competed.
>   She competed.
>   Laura and she (not *her*) competed.

> Mr. Foster gave Mollie and *me* (not *I*) a chance to play in the mixed-doubles tournament. (It is courteous to mention the other person first: "Mollie and me," NOT "me and Mollie.")
> (*Me* is one-half of the compound OBJECT of the verb *gave*.)

> Check yourself:
>   Mr. Foster gave Mollie.
>   Mr. Foster gave me.
>   Mr. Foster gave Mollie and me (not *I*).

Go with Margo and *him* (not *he*) to the flea market.
　　(*Him* is one-half of the compound OBJECT of the preposition
　　with.)

Say to yourself:
　　Go with Margo.
　　Go with him.
　　Go with Margo and him (not *he*).

Note this correct form:

The apples were divided between Tom and me.
　　(*Me*, like *Tom*, is an OBJECT of the preposition *between*.)

Study these additional examples of pronoun difficulties. Don't be fooled by the words *swimmers* and *students* in these two sentences. They do not affect the pronouns to be used.

We (not *Us*) swimmers are competing in the county champion-
ships.
　　(*We* is a SUBJECT of the verb *are competing*.)

Mr. Edmonds took *us* (not *we*) students on a tour of the Edison
home in Fort Myers.
　　(*Us* is an OBJECT of the verb *took*.)

Watch out for sentences that leave out a verb because it is understood.

Gwen is already as tall as *he* (not *him*).
　　(*He* is the SUBJECT of the understood verb *is*. Think of the
　　sentence as reading, ''Gwen is already as tall as *he is tall*.'')

Practice 1: Using the Correct Pronouns as Subjects

In each sentence, underline the correct form of the pronoun in parentheses.

1. (**We, Us**) students are late for class.
2. Maria and (**her, she**) are fond of swimming.
3. When I'm reading, nobody else can be as happy as (**I, me**).
4. Tod and (**I, me**) went to the Lakers-Celtics game.
5. Sharon, Mike, and (**he, him**) are studying together.

Practice 2: Using the Correct Pronouns as Objects

In each sentence, underline the correct form of the pronoun in parentheses.

1. Mike bought shakes for him and (**I, me**).
2. Joyce saw Greg and (**them, they**) on the bus.
3. The coach awarded letters to all of (**us, we**) members of the team.
4. We found our cat Max and (**she, her**) asleep in the hammock.
5. Play with Ralph and (**I, me**) in the band concert.

Exercise 1: Using the Correct Pronouns as Subjects or Objects

In each sentence, underline the correct form of the pronoun in parentheses.

1. (**Her, She**) and her partner will travel to Cleveland for the match.
2. Lucy prepared a hot dinner for him and (**I, me**).
3. (**Us, We**) gardeners are entering our vegetables in the county fair.
4. Sue caught sight of Lester and (**them, they**) on the bus to Lockport.
5. (**Them, They**) are applying for American citizenship as soon as possible.
6. Rover and (**I, me**) climbed Mt. Washington together.
7. When it comes to arithmetic, Don is as quick as (**her, she**).
8. Mr. Ortiz brought Nathan and (**her, she**) some homemade fudge.
9. The treasurer asked all of (**us, we**) club members to pay our back dues.
10. Joanna and (**them, they**) made all the sandwiches for the picnic.
11. At the end of the recycling drive, the chairperson of the committee praised (**us, we**) workers for our help.
12. Edwin and (**I, me**) played a strong doubles match but lost in a tiebreaker.
13. Doreen is planning a picnic for Danny and (**I, me**).
14. At the end of the school year, Sheila, Alice, and (**he, him**) were commended for academic achievement.
15. (**Us, We**) members of the Camera Club had an exhibit in the school library.
16. Rose and (**he, him**) are in the same Spanish class.
17. (**Them, They**) are the best strawberries I've ever tasted.
18. Our pen pal in Belgium wrote a newsy letter to Thomasina and (**I, me**).
19. We saw Maxine and (**he, him**) in the stands at the baseball game.
20. (**Him and I, He and I**) went on a rafting trip on the Nantahala River.

Agreement of a Pronoun with Its Antecedent

A pronoun must agree with its antecedent in number. (The word *antecedent* comes from two Latin words meaning "going before.")

A wolf is gentle with *its* young.

Its refers to *wolf*. *Wolf* is the antecedent of *its*. *Wolf* is singular. Therefore, *its* is singular. (Notice that the antecedent "goes before" the pronoun.)

Wolves are gentle with *their* young.

Their refers to *wolves*. *Wolves* is the antecedent of *their*. *Wolves* is plural. Therefore *their* is plural.

Look at these additional correct forms.

The boy from the visiting team left *his* jacket on the bus.
(*Boy* is the subject of the sentence. *Boy* is the antecedent of *his*. Both are singular.)

The girls on the tennis team take good care of *their* rackets.
(*Girls* is the subject of the sentence. *Girls* is the antecedent of *their*. Both are plural.)

Practice 3: Making Pronouns Agree with Their Antecedents

In each sentence below, write a pronoun that agrees with its antecedent.

1. A girl leaving the store stumbled and dropped _____ ice-cream cone.

2. Marilyn has a new dress, but has not worn _____ yet.

3. Michael knows that _____ will make the team.

4. Janice likes cats, but Adele hates _____ .

5. The building will have _____ roof repaired.

Indefinite Pronouns

Many problems of agreement arise with the words on the following list. They are called *indefinite pronouns*. A personal pronoun that has one of these words as an antecedent must be singular.

anybody	either	neither	one
anyone	everybody	nobody	somebody
each	everyone	no one	someone

Note the use of the correct forms.

Each of the girls must bring *her* track shoes.
(*Each* is singular. *Her* is singular.)

Everybody must report to *his* or *her* adviser.
(*Everybody* is singular. *His . . . her* with *or* is singular. Even though *everybody* "sounds" plural, it isn't. The use of *their* with *everybody* [or with any other word on the list] is incorrect in formal English.)

With *either . . . or* or *neither . . . nor*, use the nearer antecedent when choosing a pronoun.

Either *Jill* or *Claire* will bring *her* records to the dance.
(*Jill . . . Claire* is a compound subject. Since *Jill* is singular and *Claire* is also singular, the singular *her* is used.)

Neither *Norm* nor his *cousins* buy *their* groceries here.
(*Norm* is singular, but *cousins* is plural. Therefore, the plural *their* is used to agree with the nearer antecedent, *cousins*.)

Practice 4: Making Personal Pronouns Agree with Indefinite Pronouns

In each sentence below, underline the correct form of the pronoun in parentheses.

1. Someone on the girls' field hockey team forgot (**her, their**) hockey stick.
2. No one on the swimming team gave (**his or her, their**) approval to the coach's plans.
3. An elephant forms a close bond with (**its, their**) trainer.
4. Neither Boris Spassky nor Bobby Fischer kept (**his, their**) chess title for very long.
5. Everybody brought (**their, his or her**) own golf clubs.

Still another error is using a plural verb with one of the singular subjects listed on page 167, the indefinite pronouns. Note these correct forms.

Everyone at the meeting *has* a stake in the decision.
(*Everyone* is singular. *Has* is singular.)

Each of the members *was* asked to vote.
(*Each* is singular. *Was* is singular.)

Neither the *twins* nor *she wants* to go to camp this summer.
(*Twins* is plural, but *she* is singular. The singular verb, *wants*,
agrees with the nearer subject, *she*, which is also singular.)

**Some indefinite pronouns usually require a plural verb: *several, many,
both, some, few*.**

Some *were* not invited to Yolanda's party.

Many of the apples *are* still green.

Several in the stands *cheer* whenever Buck comes to bat.

Practice 5: Making Verbs Agree with Indefinite Pronouns

Underline the correct form of the verb in parentheses.

1. Either Paul or she (**are, is**) running in Saturday's marathon.
2. Nobody in the class (**are, is**) satisfied with the wall decorations.
3. A few of the audience (**is, are**) leaving before the end of the play.
4. One of the rear tires (**have, has**) gone flat.
5. Both of the children (**were, was**) late to school because the bus broke down.
6. Neither Kim nor his two sisters (**is, are**) above the age of twelve.

Possessive Pronouns

Those pesky pronouns can cause problems in yet another area—*possessives*. You have already worked with noun possessives. With nouns, you used apostrophes to show possession.

The possessives of *personal pronouns*, however, have NO apostrophes. Note the following correct forms.

Is this *yours* or *hers*?
Those books are *theirs*, not *ours*.
Where is *its* collar?

Look carefully at the last one. You have seen the word *it's*, with an apostrophe. It is a contraction of *it is*. Whenever you wonder whether *its* needs an apostrophe, simply replace *its* with *it is*. If the sentence does make sense, use an apostrophe. If it doesn't make sense (as in "Where is *it is* collar?"), *don't* use the apostrophe.

The possessives of *indefinite pronouns*, unlike personal pronouns, DO use apostrophes.

> *Somebody's* briefcase is on the kitchen table.
> *Everyone's* job is *nobody's* job.
> *No one's* opinion is more valued than Janet's.

Practice 6: Choosing Correct Possessive Pronouns

In each sentence, underline the correct form in parentheses.

1. The idea for improving the lunchroom is (**theirs, their's**).
2. The Joneses own the Chrysler. (**Ours, Our's**) is the Ford.
3. (**Its, It's**) starting to rain. Cover the chairs.
4. Ms. Maloney is (**everybodys, everybody's**) favorite history teacher.
5. The book of Emily Dickinson's poems is (**hers, her's**).
6. Is this (**someone's, someones**) science textbook?
7. The puppy limps because it injured (*its, it's*) paw.
8. The accident was (**nobodys, nobody's**) fault.
9. The Wilsons spent Thanksgiving with friends of (**theirs, their's**).
10. (**Its, It's**) time for a new ribbon in the typewriter.

Exercise 2: Choosing the Correct Pronoun

In each sentence, underline the correct form in parentheses.

1. (**We, Us**) parents are willing to help our youngsters.
2. Jane says that book is (**hers, her's**).
3. Go with John and (**I, me**) to the movie on Broadway.
4. One of the girls (**were, was**) dismissed from the chorus.
5. Neither of the boys (**plays, play**) chess.
6. (**They, Them**) are the teachers from our school.
7. Everyone on the girls' soccer team had (**her, their**) name read aloud at assembly.
8. Few brought (**his or her, their**) own pencils.
9. Between you and (**I, me**), I thought the acting was very poor.
10. Pedro and (**I, me**) liked the book very much.

Exercise 3: Writing the Correct Pronoun

Write the missing pronouns in the following sentences.

1. Alicia was in an accident. She broke _____ leg.

2. You ordered this watch and paid for it. Take it. It is _____ .

3. John and I are neighbors. _____ lives next door to me.

4. Linda and Sue are our friends. We like _____ very much.

5. The ball fell right into your hands, but you could not hold _____ .

6. Thelma gave Johnny the book. _____ had bought it especially for _____ .

7. One of the boys played in every game. _____ was exhausted.

8. The coach and the team prepared for the game. _____ still lost.

9. Did you know the last answer? _____ was easy, wasn't it?

10. Mr. and Mrs. Lee made the last payment on their car. Now it belongs to _____ .

6. Problems with Punctuation

A complete list of the rules of punctuation would fill a small book. Fortunately, you don't have to learn them all. Mastery of a few basic rules will help you avoid most of the pitfalls in punctuating sentences. The following review covers the main points.

End Punctuation

Every sentence ends with a period, a question mark, or an exclamation point.

Statement:	A Pekingese has a longer life expectancy than a Saint Bernard.
Command:	Read this book about how to repair a faucet.
Polite request:	May I hear from you soon.
Question:	Have you ever visited Acadia National Park**?**
Strong feeling:	What a wonderful time we had at Sea World!

Practice 1: Writing Correct End Punctuation

Copy these sentences, writing the proper end punctuation marks.

1. Where did you put the hammer

   _____

2. Please pass the butter

   _____

3. How beautiful that sunset is

   _____

4. Why didn't you cut the lawn

   _____

5. The word *paper* comes from the Egyptian word for papyrus

   _____

The period is also used after abbreviations and most initials.

Dr. R. J. Lowenherz   P.M.   Jr.   R.S.V.P.

The Comma

The comma has many uses. Three important uses that you should review are commas in a series; commas to show interrupters; and commas in letters, dates, and addresses.

Commas in a Series

Use a comma to separate items in a series.

At camp we hiked, swam, golfed, and played softball.

My brother collects stamps, coins, and picture postcards.

Sue looked for the tickets on the desk, in the desk drawer, and on the dresser.

(Some writers omit the comma before the *and*. This can be confusing in some sentences, however. The safest practice is to include the final comma in all such sentences.)

When more than one adjective precedes a noun, use a comma for a pause.

The gloomy, isolated mansion stood at the edge of a cliff. (Pause after *gloomy*.)

Oliver was a lively young dog. (No pause.)

Commas to Show Interrupters

Use a pair of commas to enclose most interrupting words or expressions.

Our Mr. Pooch, like most beagles, is a friendly dog.

Siamese cats, on the other hand, are more reserved.

Tallahassee, not Miami, is the capital of Florida.

I'm surprised, Madge, that you believe his story.

She admitted that, yes, she could see his point of view.

The route through Evansville is, according to Jack, the best route to Janet's house.

The old car, rusted and dented, was not worth fixing.

When an interrupter comes at the beginning or at the end of a sentence, only one comma is needed.

Like most beagles, our Mr. Pooch is a friendly dog.

On the other hand, Siamese cats are more reserved.

The capital of Florida is Tallahassee, not Miami.

I'm surprised that you believe his story, Madge.

Yes, I admit that I can see your point of view.

Paul disagrees, however.

Rusted and dented, the old car was not worth fixing.

Use a comma to enclose most appositives. An appositive explains the noun or pronoun it follows. It is most commonly a noun.

> Songhay, an African *kingdom* in the late 1400s, was larger than western Europe.

> The Antarctic waters, *fertilizer* for the rest of the world, help support life in the other oceans.

Adjectives sometimes appear in the appositive position.

> The old house, *grim* and *foreboding*, lowered over Main Street.

> Spiders, *unpopular* but *essential*, destroy a hundred times their number in insects.

Use commas to enclose appositives preceded by *or*.

> The avocado, or *alligator pear*, was first cultivated by the Aztecs.

Practice 2: Punctuating Correctly

Copy these sentences, adding all needed punctuation. (Notice that end punctuation must be added, too.)

1. Saturday was a dark cold dreary day

_____

2. The leopard like the lion is an outstanding hunter

_____

3. No I strongly object to your remarks

_____

4. Did you ever find your missing notebook Tammy

_____

5. Blue not red is Sue's favorite color

_____

6. Marilyn however prefers green especially light green

_____

7. Vince is a fine swimmer diver golfer and soccer player

_____

8. Are you aware that George Washington our first President served two terms

_____

9. William Henry Harrison on the other hand served only a month

_____

10. The rutabaga or yellow turnip is my favorite vegetable

_____

Exercise 1: Punctuating Correctly

Copy these sentences, adding all needed punctuation. (Notice that end punctuation must also be added.)

1. The coffee tree a native of Africa still grows wild in Ethiopia and Liberia

_____

_____

2. This summer we hiked in Pisgah National Forest ate lunch by woodland waterfalls and enjoyed views from mountaintops

_____

_____

3. I'm grateful to you Stewart and Betsy for taping that program we wanted to see

_____

_____

4. The sassafras unlike most trees has three different and distinct leaf patterns

_____

_____

5. Sandra please hand me that hammer

_____

_____

6. On our trip we visited Banff Lake Louise and Jasper

_____

_____

7. The mountain range stark and majestic was outlined against the twilight sky

_____

_____

8. Where did you put the teapot Lonnie

_____

_____

9. Alfred Nobel the inventor of dynamite also invented plywood

_____

_____

10. Falling temperatures not wind are threatening the orange crop

_____

_____

Commas in Letters, Dates, and Addresses

1. When dates and addresses occur within sentences, you punctuate them as in the following examples.

> Write to Meg Acieri, 908 Beechwood Drive, Hendersonville, NC 28739.
> (Notice that there is no comma between the name of the state and the ZIP code.)

> Mr. Blakiston was born on June 19, 1917, in Chicago, IL.
> (Notice that there is a comma after the year as well as in front of it.)

2. When dates and addresses appear in the heading or the inside address of a letter, you punctuate them like this:

33 Barrett Street
Elmira, NY 14904
August 22, 19--

Mr. Stephen Dorney
La Bravura Drive
Beverly Hills, CA 90213

The U.S. Postal Service recommends two-letter state abbreviations for addressing letters. These abbreviations have no periods (*NY*, not *N.Y.*), and they often differ from traditional abbreviations (*CA*, not *Cal.* or *Calif.*). If you are unsure of the two-letter abbreviation, write out the state name. A list of official postal abbreviations follows.

Alabama	AL	Kentucky	KY	Ohio	OH
Alaska	AK	Louisiana	LA	Oklahoma	OK
Arizona	AZ	Maine	ME	Oregon	OR
Arkansas	AR	Maryland	MD	Pennsylvania	PA
California	CA	Massachusetts	MA	Puerto Rico	PR
Colorado	CO	Michigan	MI	Rhode Island	RI
Connecticut	CT	Minnesota	MN	South Carolina	SC
Delaware	DE	Mississippi	MS	South Dakota	SD
Dist. of Col.	DC	Missouri	MO	Tennessee	TN
Florida	FL	Montana	MT	Texas	TX
Georgia	GA	Nebraska	NE	Utah	UT
Guam	GU	Nevada	NV	Vermont	VT
Hawaii	HI	New Hampshire	NH	Virginia	VA
Idaho	ID	New Jersey	NJ	Virgin Islands	VI
Illinois	IL	New Mexico	NM	Washington	WA
Indiana	IN	New York	NY	West Virginia	WV
Iowa	IA	North Carolina	NC	Wisconsin	WI
Kansas	KS	North Dakota	ND	Wyoming	WY

3. Use a comma after the salutation of a friendly letter and the complimentary close of all letters. (See page 75.)

Dear Carole,   Sincerely,

Dear Uncle Frank,   Very truly yours,

4. Use a colon after the salutation of a business letter.

Gentlemen: Dear Ms. Valenzuela:

(For the proper form of a business letter, see pages 74–76.)

Practice 3: Punctuating Dates and Addresses

Copy these sentences, adding all needed punctuation. (Notice that end punctuation must also be added.)

1. The Massachusetts Bureau of Markets is now located at 100 Cambridge Street Boston MA 02202

2. Was it July 16 1969 when the *Apollo 11* lunar expedition set out for the moon

_____

_____

3. The United Negro College Fund has offices at 500 East 62 Street New York NY 10001

_____

_____

4. Write to the Lyndon B. Johnson National Historical Park P.O. Box 329 Johnson City TX 78636

_____

_____

5. John Adams and Thomas Jefferson died on July 4 1826 exactly fifty years after signing the Declaration of Independence

_____

_____

Exercise 2

Copy these sentences, adding all needed punctuation. (Notice that end punctuation must also be added.)

1. On May 5 1961 Alan B Shepard Jr became the first American in space

_____

_____

2. My brother lives at 15 Dogwood Circle Boynton Beach FL 33462

_____

_____

3. John F Kennedy was born on May 29 1917 and became President of the United States at the age of 43

_____

_____

4. Sandra ordered a book from Carter Publications 335 Hudson Street New York NY 10013

_____

_____

5. Neil Armstrong US astronaut first walked on the moon July 20 1969

_____

_____

Quotation Marks

A direct quotation shows the speaker's exact words. An indirect quotation does not.

Direct quotation: Dad said, "You can go to camp this summer." (Quotation marks needed)

Indirect quotation: Dad said that I can go to camp this summer. (No quotation marks)

Quotation marks always go in pairs. If you have opening quotation marks, you must have closing quotation marks.

Ellen said, "I'm taking the school bus home."

"I'm taking the school bus home," Ellen said.

"When do you leave?" asked Carlos.

Carlos asked, "When do you leave?"

"I hope," said Fran, "that you remember to take your science book home."

"When do we eat?" Billy asked. "I'm hungry."

Did Billy say, "I'm hungry"?
  (The entire sentence is a question.)

"I had never seen a snow leopard before," Maureen said. "Had you?"

Practice 4: Punctuating Quotations

Copy the following sentences. Add all needed punctuation.

1. Let's go fishing in Murray Creek suggested Alice

_____

2. Ron replied I promised Dad I'd trim the hedge

_____

3. What book did you choose for a report asked Mr. Peterson

_____

4. That was a great play yelled Paul

_____

5. It was the first time said Alice that I've thrown the ball that far

_____

_____

Exercise 3

Copy the following sentences. Add all needed punctuation.

1. How did ragtime music start asked Donna

_____

_____

2. The coach stopped Hal and asked are you trying out for the team

_____

_____

3. Work is the best method devised for killing time said William Feather

_____

_____

4. Education is what remains said Lord Halifax when we have forgotten all that we have been taught

_____

_____

5. I must follow the people said Benjamin Disraeli Am I not their leader (Why is *am* capitalized?)

_____

_____

Punctuating Titles

In general, use quotation marks around the titles of short works—a short story, an essay, a song, a magazine article, or the chapter of a book. Underline the titles of longer works—a book, a film, a magazine, or a newspaper. (In printed material, underlined words appear in *italics*.)

"I Am Born" is the title of a chapter in *David Copperfield* by Charles Dickens.

"On Running After One's Hat" is a classic essay by G. K. Chesterton.

"Memphis" is my favorite song from the Statler Brothers' album *Funny, Familiar, Forgotten Feelings*.

I've seen the movie *Back to the Future* at least five times.

TV Guide is one of the most successful magazines ever published.

The Newark *Star-Ledger* publishes different editions for different counties.
(Be careful to capitalize the exact name of the newspaper. Usually *the* is not capitalized as part of the name, but in *The New York Times* it is. Sometimes the name of the city is part of the name of the paper, as in the *Chicago Sun-Times*, and sometimes it isn't.)

Practice 5: Writing Titles

Copy the following sentences. Punctuate each correctly.

1. The Red Badge of Courage is the book I have decided to read

   _____

2. The newspaper Newsday has many readers, but not as many as the Times

   _____

3. Did you see The Color Purple

   _____

4. She wrote a story called After Dark which was published in Seventeen magazine

   _____

5. Young Love was my mother's favorite song

   _____

Exercise 4

Copy these sentences, adding all needed punctuation.

1. Did you go to the Dolphins games asked Mr. Gomez

   _____

   _____

2. Caroline went to see Rocky IV in Joplin MO

_____

_____

3. Janice bought new shoes sweaters skirts and jeans

_____

_____

4. I wonder said Janie where I put my new sunglasses

_____

_____

5. No I want you to do your homework first said her mother

_____

_____

6. James said that his new address would be 21330 Fronthill Avenue Torrance CA 90505

_____

_____

7. My brother was born October 22 1984 on a Sunday

_____

_____

8. Sometimes it is confusing said Mr. Thomas but the New York Giants play their home games in New Jersey

_____

_____

9. I'm surprised Rick that you did not bring your friend

_____

_____

10. I read an article called Without Fear in Time magazine

_____

_____

Exercise 5

Each of the sentences below contains an underlined part. There are four suggested answers. Write the letter of the correct answer on the line at the right.

1. <u>Oh its</u> a long time until the end of the movie.

   (*a*) Correct as is   (*b*) Oh, its'
   (*c*) Oh, its   (*d*) Oh, it's   1. _____

2. "Will you let me use the <u>car" Jim asked?</u>

   (*a*) Correct as is   (*b*) car?" Jim asked.
   (*c*) car," Jim asked?   (*d*) car, Jim asked.   2. _____

3. Did you <u>read Tom Sawyer.</u>

   (*a*) Correct as is   (*b*) read, "Tom Sawyer"
   (*c*) read *Tom Sawyer*?   (*d*) read Tom Sawyer?   3. _____

4. It was <u>June 12, 1986 when</u> we went on the trip.

   (*a*) Correct as is   (*b*) June 12, 1986, when
   (*c*) June 12 1986 when   (*d*) June, 12, 1986, when   4. _____

5. <u>What said Joey did</u> you mean by that remark?"

   (*a*) Correct as is   (*b*) "What," said Joey, "did
   (*c*) "What," said Joey "did   (*d*) What said, Joey, Did   5. _____

7. Problems with Capitalization

The following review summarizes the important rules of capitalization.

In Letters

Capitalize the first word and all nouns in the *salutation*.

Dear James,   Dear Mr. Patterson:
Dear Aunt Jane,   Dear Miss McCloud:

Capitalize only the first word in the *complimentary close*.

Your friend,   Very truly yours,
Your niece,   Cordially yours,

In Quotations

A direct quotation begins with a capital letter.

Elizabeth Barrett Browning wrote, ''How do I love thee?''

When a one-sentence quotation is interrupted, however, the second part does not start with a capital.

''Can anyone,'' the announcer asked, ''name that tune?''

Review pages 179–180 for other examples of the capitalization of quotations.

First Words

Capitalize the first word of a complete sentence, the comments of each new speaker in conversation, and each line of poetry or verse.

Sentence: The antelope survives on dry plains.

Conversation: ''It is not cold which makes me shiver,'' said the woman in a low voice.
''What, then?''
''It is fear, Mr. Holmes. It is terror.''
—from Arthur Conan Doyle's ''The Adventure of the Speckled Band''

Poetry: **T**he pedigree of honey
        Does not concern the bee;
   A clover, any time, to him
     Is aristocracy.
         —Emily Dickinson

Proper Nouns and Proper Adjectives

Capitalize proper nouns, their abbreviations, and proper adjectives derived from proper nouns.

Proper noun: **New M**exico

Abbreviation: **N.M**. (or NM, the postal abbreviation)

Proper adjective: **New M**exican (as in *New Mexican* art)

Practice 1: Capitalizing Correctly

A. Copy the following, adding needed capitals.

1. dear mr. keane: _____

2. your friend,   _____

3. dear henry,   _____

4. sincerely yours,   _____

5. dear mr. thomas: _____

6. yours very truly,   _____

B. Copy the following, and capitalize each sentence correctly.

1. Once Dan Rather ended his newscast by saying, ''courage.''

_____

_____

2. ''Do you know,'' asked the teacher, ''Who serves as the Secretary of State?''

_____

_____

3. ''Please do your homework before you go out,'' Said her mother.

_____

_____

C. Correctly capitalize the following conversation.

"where were you born?" asked the interviewer.
marian said, "i was born in columbus, ohio."
"when did you move to north carolina?"
"in 1990, when my father accepted his new job here."

_____

_____

_____

_____

Exercise 1: Capitalizing Correctly

Copy the following, and capitalize each sentence correctly.

1. susie began her letter, "dear aunt olivia."

_____

_____

2. mark twain said, "if you tell the truth, you don't have to remember anything."

_____

_____

3. "why don't you enroll in typing next semester?" suggested mrs. esposito.

_____

_____

4. "opportunity," said peter drucker, "only knocks on the doors of those who deserve it."

_____

_____

5. will rogers said, "don't let yesterday use up too much of today."

_____

_____

Here are some specific kinds of proper nouns that require capital letters.

Names of particular persons, real or imaginary

> Linda, Jeremy, Dolly Parton, Tom Selleck, Sandra Day O'Connor, James Bond, Lois Lane

Geographical names

> Australia, New Jersey, Palm Beach County, Yosemite National Park, Fifth Avenue

Titles of organizations, companies, and buildings

> Kiwanis Club, National Audubon Society, Ford Motor Company, World Trade Center, Riverside Cathedral

Political parties, nations, religions, government bodies

> Republican, Democrat, France, Roman Catholic, Protestant, Hebrew, Senate, Department of the Interior

Titles of persons showing office, rank, profession

> President Roosevelt, General Marshall, Dr. Reed

Names of planets, satellites, stars, and constellations

> Jupiter, Ganymede, Sirius, the Big Dipper
> (The words *sun*, *earth*, and *moon* are not usually capitalized.)

Names of days of the week, months, holidays

> Thursday, March, Independence Day
> (The names of the seasons are not capitalized.)

Titles

> *Gone with the Wind*, *Better Homes and Gardens*, ''The Night the Ghost Got In''
> (Articles—*a, an, the*—prepositions, and conjunctions are not capitalized unless they occur at the beginning or end of a title.)

Brand names

> Campbell's soups, Pepperidge Farm bread, Andy Boy broccoli

Names referring to God, the Bible, or religions

> the Almighty, Exodus, the Old Testament, Christianity, Buddhism

There are three kinds of items that require extra thought if you are to capitalize them correctly.

Sections of the country

the **S**outheast, the **N**orthwest, the **S**outhwest

Do <u>not</u> capitalize these words if they are merely compass points:

Philadelphia lies southwest of New York City.

Family relationships

Father, **S**is, **C**ousin **G**ene, **A**unt **G**loria, **G**randpa

Do <u>not</u> capitalize these family titles unless they are used before a name (**U**ncle **S**id) or as a name (Hi, **M**om):

My sister, cousin, and aunt visited Duke Gardens.

School subjects: languages and numbered courses

English, **F**rench, **S**panish, **G**erman, **M**echanical **D**rawing 2, **S**ocial **S**tudies 3, **M**athematics 4

Do <u>not</u> capitalize the names of unnumbered courses except for languages.

I'm taking mechanical drawing, social studies, mathematics, and **G**erman in the fall.

Practice 2

Draw a circle around each letter that should be capitalized.

1. my uncle in london
2. the republican candidate
3. english and history
4. the planet saturn
5. fourth of july holiday

6. john jay high school
7. *raiders of the lost ark*
8. grandma and aunt louise
9. in the southwest near phoenix
10. fire island national seashore

Exercise 2

A. Copy these sentences, adding needed capitals.

1. mayor selkirk spoke at the meeting of the rotary club.

_____

_____

2. the blue ridge parkway winds through some of the most beautiful mountain scenery in the east.

_____

_____

3. my sister has already taken spanish and french in high school.

_____

4. a chrysler assembly plant is being built at the corner of spring street and linden boulevard.

_____

_____

5. the only continent my uncle hasn't visited is antarctica.

_____

6. the empire state building is still a major tourist attraction in new york city.

_____

_____

7. the department of agriculture has charge of our national forests.

_____

_____

8. i saw venus and jupiter in the sky at twilight on labor day.

_____

_____

9. the first two books of the old testament are genesis and exodus.

_____

_____

10. my cousin, major andrea langer, has just returned from a tour of duty in the northwest.

_____

_____

B. Copy the following poem, adding needed capitals.

> and the night shall be filled with music,
>   and the cares that infest the day
> shall fold their tents like the arabs,
>   and as silently steal away.
>   —Henry Wadsworth Longfellow

_____

_____

_____

_____

_____

8. Problems with Spelling

You are more likely to misspell common words than uncommon ones. That is because you probably look up the spellings of hard words, while you assume that you know how to spell the easy ones.

Seventy-six Hard/Easy Words

The words in the following list are among the most commonly used in English. Yet they are frequently misspelled. Review them and master them.

ache	certain	heard	realize
acquaint	character	hospital	really
across	coming	immediately	says
agreeable	committee	instead	scene
all right	cough	knew	since
almost	course	knowledge	speech
always	disappear	library	straight
among	disappoint	meant	studying
another	doctor	minute	success
asked	doesn't	necessary	surely
athletic	dropped	occasion	surprise
beautiful	enough	occurred	though
before	every	often	thought
believe	exception	once	threw
benefit	excitement	piece	together
boundary	experience	pleasant	toward
break	friend	principal [school]	until
built	grammar	privilege	which
captain	having	probably	woman

Practice 1: Spelling Correctly

In each sentence below, there is a partially spelled word. Write the complete word in the space at the right.

1. When Jan won the contest, there was a lot of **exci____ment** at our house.   1. _____

2. It is not **nec_____ry** to answer my letter.   2. _____

3. The teacher appointed a **com_____tee** to study the problem.   3. _____

4. I'll meet you in the **lib_____y.**   4. _____

5. Jack is having a **su_____rise** party for Gilda.   5. _____

6. The new rules will **ben_____it** everyone in the class.

6. _____

7. **Al_____ight,** I'll help with the refreshments at the party.

7. _____

8. Mr. Parker wants those reports **im_____ diately,** not tomorrow.

8. _____

9. I think the most interesting **char_____er** in *David Copperfield* is Mr. Micawber.

9. _____

10. I'm not **cert_____n,** but I think Andy will take Ruth to the dance.

10. _____

Exercise 1: Spelling Correctly

In each sentence below, there is a partially spelled word. Write the complete word in the space at the right.

1. Is there a difference between **kno_____ge** and wisdom?

1. _____

2. Gene has scholastic as well as **ath_____tic** skills.

2. _____

3. The **princip_____** of our school once ran in the Olympics.

3. _____

4. Mom says Dad is her best **fr_____nd.**

4. _____

5. I hope my cold **dis_____p_____ears** before the picnic.

5. _____

6. I've been **stud_____ng** for the test since March.

6. _____

7. Does every rule have an **ex_____ption?**

7. _____

8. The **capt_____n** of the soccer team can run 100 yards in 10 seconds.

8. _____

9. Come to the play; don't **dis_____point** us.

9. _____

10. My graduation will be an important **oc_____ sion.**

10. _____

Words Commonly Used in Letter Writing

This list contains words that are often misspelled in letters.

advertisement	business	choose	coupon
appreciate	busy	clothes	decided
beginning	buy	color	delivery

describe	magazine	recommend	Thursday
different	ninety, ninth	response	Tuesday
February	prompt	secretary	Wednesday
first	purchased	separate	wholesale
forty, fourth	receive	sincerely	writing

Practice 2

In the sentences below, there are partially spelled words. Fill in the missing letters.

1. I am responding to your **advert_____ment** in the *Post*.

2. I'll **ap_____ciate** an early reply to this letter.

3. As the **sec_____ry** of our English class, I am **writ_____ng** to invite you to our Fun Fair.

4. The meeting of the Shutter Club is held on the first **Wed_____ay** of each month.

5. Could you **rec_____end** a computer for personal use?

6. I can meet you at the close of **bu_____ess** on **T_____day** or **T_____day**.

7. I expected **deli_____ry** by the first of the month, but the parcel has not yet arrived.

8. I sent two **sep_____te** orders, which have somehow become mixed up.

9. I was pleased to **re_____ve** your **pro_____t** reply.

10. We intend to order your **magaz_____** in **Feb_____ry**.

Exercise 2

In the sentences below, there are partially spelled words. Fill in the missing letters.

1. How would you **des_____be** the taste of eggplant?

2. Try to make the **beg_____ng** of your composition particularly interesting.

3. There is a saying, ''Give a job to a **bu_____y** person.''

4. For lunch I **rec_____end** the chicken-salad sandwich.

5. I **sinc_____ly** hope your **resp_____e** to the invitation is positive.

Words Often Confused

Note the correct spelling of the words in boldfaced type.

I'll **accept** every package **except** the one with the torn wrapping.

We looked at old pictures. **Then** Peter was taller **than** Norm.

She's **too** late **to** enter the race.

Because of the trees all around, our house is **quite quiet**.

Your necklace is **loose**. Don't **lose** it.

Whether we go or not depends on the **weather**.

It's time to give the hamster **its** lunch.

You're leading **your** opponent in the election.

They're going **there** with **their** hopes high.

Where can I **wear** this formal gown?

Practice 3

In each sentence, underline the correct spelling.

1. I think Val's report was (**quiet, quite**) interesting.

2. (**Their, There**) is no reason for becoming discouraged.

3. (**Wear, Where**) did you put the ice skates?

4. I hope I didn't (**loose, lose**) my bracelet. I can't find it anywhere.

5. Please (**accept, except**) our congratulations for the honor you have won.

6. That perky spaniel is older (**than, then**) that weary-looking terrier.

7. I don't know (**weather, whether**) I'll be able to finish my report in time.

8. Ginny was glad to learn that (**your, you're**) coming to the basketball game.

9. Sometimes Marty can be just (**to, too**) relaxed.

10. (**It's, Its**) your move.

Exercise 3

In each sentence, underline the correct spelling.

1. (**Its, It's**) (**to, too**) early to leave for the party.

2. Everyone in the class is shorter (**than, then**) Paul (**accept, except**) Mel.

3. (**Weather, Whether**) or not we buy the new house depends on how (**quiet, quite**) the neighborhood is.

4. (**Your, You're**) lucky you didn't (**loose, lose**) the scarf you like so much.

5. (**Their, There, They're**) going to (**wear, where**) the clown outfits to Nathaniel's birthday party.

Seven Helpful Spelling Rules

These simple rules can help you to spell a great many words correctly.

1. **Ei, Ie.** Put **i** before **e** except after **c**, or when sounded like **a** as in *neighbor* and *weigh*.

> **i** before **e**:   bel**ie**ve, ch**ie**f, n**ie**ce, f**ie**ld, sh**ie**ld
> except after **c**:   **cei**ling, re**cei**ve, de**cei**t, con**cei**t, per**cei**ve
> sounded like **a**:   w**ei**ght, v**ei**l, v**ei**n, r**ei**gn, r**ei**n
> *Exceptions:*   for**ei**gner, l**ei**sure, **ei**ther, n**ei**ther, h**ei**ght

Practice 4

Fill in the missing letters, and write the complete word at the right.

1. Please answer **br_____fly.**   1. _____
2. How much do the potatoes **w_____gh**?   2. _____
3. Frank is your **n_____ghbor.**   3. _____
4. What is your **h_____ght**?   4. _____
5. We installed a **c_____ling** fan.   5. _____

2. **Ly.** Keep the original **l** when adding **ly** to a word ending in **l**.

> actual**l**y, beautiful**l**y, cheerful**l**y, final**l**y, real**l**y

Exercise 4

Fill in the missing letters, and write the complete word at the right.

1. The **r_____gn** of Queen Victoria was one of the longest in history.   1. _____
2. **N_____ther** answer is correct.   2. _____
3. May I have a **p_____ce** of cherry pie?   3. _____
4. Did you **rec_____ve** my card from Yellowstone?   4. _____
5. A person's use of **l_____sure** is a key to his or her character.   5. _____

Practice 5

Fill in the missing letters, and write the complete word at the right.

1. Look **carefu_____y** before crossing the street.   1. _____

2. Lena strolled **casua_____y** through the mall.   2. _____

3. Attendance was **unusua_____y** large today.   3. _____

4. The host greeted his guests **cordia_____y.**   4. _____

5. That mischievous child tossed my book into the lake **intentiona_____y.**   5. _____

Exercise 5

Fill in the missing letters, and write the complete word at the right.

1. Our car was **fu_____y** packed.   1. _____

2. I tripped **accidenta_____y.**   2. _____

3. We accepted the advice **gratefu_____y.**   3. _____

4. I couldn't believe we had **actua_____y** arrived.   4. _____

5. Mona greeted the guests **cheerfu_____y.**   5. _____

3. Final E Before Vowel. Drop silent **e** before a suffix beginning with a vowel.

admir∉able, argu∉ing, larg∉est, enclos∉ing, scarc∉ity

Practice 6

Fill in the missing letters, and write the complete word at the right.

1. **Advers_____ty** is no stranger to some unfortunate people.   1. _____

2. This detergent made my white shirt look even **whit_____r.**   2. _____

3. The network is **experienc_____g** technical difficulties.   3. _____

4. He plays wide **receiv_____r** on the team.   4. _____

5. Vacations are very **desir_____ble.**   5. _____

Exercise 6

Fill in the missing letters, and write the complete word at the right.

1. The players were **argu_____g** over the umpire's decision.

    1. _____

2. Maxine was **practic_____g** her guitar.

    2. _____

3. Fran has an **admir_____le** record in French.

    3. _____

4. Bud's story is **unbeliev_____le**.

    4. _____

5. Our cat kept **interfer_____g** with my homework.

    5. _____

4. Final E Before Consonant. Keep final silent **e** before a suffix beginning with a consonant.

amaz**e**ment, aton**e**ment, hop**e**ful, fortunat**e**ly, us**e**ful

Exceptions: acknowledgment, argument, awful, duly, judgment, ninth, truly, wholly

Practice 7

Fill in the missing letters, and write the complete word at the right.

1. There was a lot of **excit_____ment** about the game.

    1. _____

2. Jerry is **hop_____lessly** behind in his school-work; but now that he is well again, he expects to catch up.

    2. _____

3. She was told to be very **car_____ful** with the car.

    3. _____

4. **Saf_____ty** first!

    4. _____

5. Lucy looks **lov_____ly** in her new gown.

    5. _____

Exercise 7

Fill in the missing letters, and write the complete word at the right.

1. **Nin_____een** planes were ahead of us on the Atlanta runway.

    1. _____

2. Failing to recycle is **wast_____ul**.

    2. _____

3. Hiking provides **peac_____ul** settings.

    3. _____

4. June **car_____ully** opened the package.

    4. _____

5. **Fortunat_____y** I had an extra set of keys.

    5. _____

5. **Final Y.** If final **y** is preceded by a consonant, change **y** to **i** when you add a suffix.

> app**ly** + ed = applied (**Y** changed to **i**.)
> friend**ly** + er = friendlier
> noi**sy** + est = noisiest

But notice the following forms.

> apply + ing = appl**y**ing
>   (**Y** does not change to **i** if the suffix begins with **i**.)
> play + er = pla**y**er
>   (**Y** does not change to **i** if **y** is preceded by a vowel.)

Practice 8

Fill in the missing letters, and write the complete word at the right.

1. The two girls **hurr_____d** home after school.   1. _____

2. The paint is **dr_____ng** very fast.   2. _____

3. This holiday, Mother is **bus_____er** than ever.   3. _____

4. The secretary has **suppl_____** us with paper.   4. _____

5. The company was slow in **repl_____ng** to my letter.   5. _____

6. Father asked to have the car **spra_____ed.**   6. _____

6. **Doubling Final Consonant—One-Syllable Words.** Note the following correct forms. Each final consonant is preceded by a single vowel.

> bat + er = ba**tt**er
>   (The final consonant, **t**, is doubled.)
> big + est = bi**gg**est
> drop + ing = dro**pp**ing
> grin + ed = gri**nn**ed

What happens when the final consonant is preceded by more than one vowel?

> beat + en = bea**t**en
>   (The final consonant, **t**, is not doubled.)
> sail + ed = sailed
> dream + er = drea**m**er
> fool + ish = foolish
> foam + ing = foa**m**ing

Exercise 8

Fill in the missing letters, and write the complete word at the right.

1. Nan **accompan_____d** Aunt Lucy to the airport.   1. _____

2. Ed has never been **happ_____r**.   2. _____

3. Marcy **stud_____d** all night.   3. _____

4. We **carr_____d** our hand luggage to the plane.   4. _____

5. Al solved that difficult third problem **eas_____ ly**.   5. _____

Practice 9

Fill in the missing letters, and write the complete word at the right.

1. The lost puppy was **roa_____ing** the street.   1. _____

2. Jessie was the last **swi_____er** to reach the raft.   2. _____

3. She was **pla_____ing** to go to the store.   3. _____

4. The rain **sto_____ed** and the sun shone again.   4. _____

5. Elizabeth **fail_____d** to return the call.   5. _____

Exercise 9

Fill in the missing letters, and write the complete word at the right.

1. The receiver **drop_____d** the ball in the end zone.   1. _____

2. Our neighbor **help_____d** us with the painting.   2. _____

3. Is that package **wrap_____d** securely?   3. _____

4. Without water, the flowers **droop_____d**.   4. _____

5. The wood under the front porch steps had **rot_____d**.   5. _____

7. **Doubling Final Consonant—Words of More Than One Syllable.** If a word has more than one syllable and the accent is on the last syllable, the same rule applies as for a one-syllable word.

> commit + ed = commi**tt**ed
>   (The accent is on the last syllable—**t** is doubled.)
> control + ing = contro**ll**ing
> equip + ed = equi**pp**ed
> propel + er = prope**ll**er
> refer + ed = refe**rr**ed

What happens if the word is not accented on the last syllable?

refer + ence = reference
(The accent is not on **er**; **r** is not doubled.)

Practice 10

Fill in the missing letters, and write the complete word at the right.

1. Don **prefe**_____**ed** another doctor.   1. _____

2. The accident was **regre**_____**able**.   2. _____

3. Who **benefi**_____**ed** from the donation?   3. _____

4. The movie **diffe**_____**ed** from the book.   4. _____

5. She is **exce**_____**ing** in music.   5. _____

Exercise 10

Fill in the missing letters, and write the complete word at the right.

1. **Control**_____**ng** a spirited horse isn't easy.   1. _____

2. Those **swim**_____**rs** are trying out for the Olympic team.   2. _____

3. Marcus **offer**_____**d** to run first in the half-mile relay.   3. _____

4. For trekking in Nepal, a hiker must be well **equip**_____**d**.   4. _____

5. Nadine has always **excel**_____**d** in craft work. 5. _____

Exercise 11

Applying all the spelling rules you have learned, fill in the missing letters in the sentences below.

1. Priscilla wore a colorful **handkerch**_____**f** as a head covering.

2. We **usu**_____**y** visit Grandma once a month.

3. That tower is **interfe**_____**ng** with television reception.

4. There were **nin**_____**een** members on our last hike.

5. We have **occup**_____**ed** our present house for three months.

6. The Stage Squad is **plan**_____**ng** a post-performance party.

7. Martha was a good piano player, but Louise **excel**_____**d** on the violin.

8. The next **meet**_____**g** of the Stamp Club will be held on Saturday.

9. In *Othello*, Iago **dec_____ves** his trusting friend.

10. Have you ever **tr_____ed** to play badminton?

11. When the rookie **fina_____y** hit a home run, the spectators gave him a standing ovation.

12. I am **enclos_____ng** a photograph.

13. Computers are very **us_____ful.**

14. Rhonda is **friend_____r** than Sally.

15. Mark is the next **ba_____er** at the plate.

Contractions

A *contraction* is a word that has been shortened by omitting one or more letters. Insert an apostrophe where one or more letters are left out in a word. In writing contractions, don't add a letter and don't change the letters around.

she + is = she's	we + are = we're
he + will = he'll	can + not = can't
they + have = they've	I + would = I'd

Exception: will + not = won't

Don't put an apostrophe in the wrong place:

Wrong:	have'nt	could'nt	do'nt
Right:	haven't	couldn't	don't
Remember:	The possessives of personal pronouns do not have apostrophes (pages 169–170).		

Exercise 12

Write the correct contraction for each word group.

1. that + is	_____	6. has + not	_____
2. you + have	_____	7. we + will	_____
3. did + not	_____	8. do + not	_____
4. it + is	_____	9. I + am	_____
5. does + not	_____	10. they + are	_____

PART III

Multiple-Choice Tests

Note: The italicized numbers in parentheses in tests A–F, H, and I refer to text pages where you can find help in answering the questions.

A. In each of the following sentences, an underlined portion may be correct or incorrect. Circle the letter of the answer you consider correct.

(164–166) 1. Mom divided the remaining cookies <u>between Alice and I.</u>

    A. between Alice and I.
    B. between I and Alice.
    C. between Alice and me.
    D. between me and Alice.

(152–153, 161) 2. Fletcher <u>done unusually good</u> on the math test.

    A. done unusually good
    B. did unusually good
    C. done unusually well
    D. did unusually well

(188–189) 3. Next year, I plan to take <u>Spanish, English, geometry, and history.</u>

    A. Spanish, English, geometry, and history.
    B. Spanish, English, geometry, and History.
    C. Spanish, English, Geometry, and History.
    D. Spanish, english, geometry, and history.

(138–142) 4. I can't find my <u>catcher's mitt have you seen it?</u>

    A. catcher's mitt have you seen it?
    B. catcher's mitt, have you seen it?
    C. catcher's mitt. Have you seen it?
    D. catcher's mitt? Have you seen it?

(154–158, 194) 5. At least one of the apples <u>weren't too ripe.</u>

    A. weren't too ripe.
    B. wasn't too ripe.
    C. weren't to ripe.
    D. wasn't to ripe.

(145, 154–
158)   6. The upper <u>gum of sheep is toothless</u>.

    A. gum of sheep is toothless.
    B. gums of sheep is toothless.
    C. gum of sheep are toothless.
    D. gum of sheeps is toothless.

(176–177)   7. Our new address is 553 Peters <u>Boulevard, Brightwaters New York 11718</u>.

    A. Boulevard, Brightwaters New York 11718.
    B. Boulevard, Brightwaters, New York, 11718.
    C. Boulevard; Brightwaters, New York 11718.
    D. Boulevard, Brightwaters, New York 11718.

(163)   8. <u>That there VCR is the latest</u> on the market.

    A. That there VCR is the latest
    B. That VCR is the latest
    C. That VCR is the most latest
    D. That there VCR is the most latest

(162)   9. I <u>can't read anything</u> without my reading glasses.

    A. can't read anything
    B. can't read nothing
    C. cant read anything
    D. cant read nothing

(149–152)   10. I <u>seen the game, and then I go</u> home directly.

    A. seen the game, and then I go
    B. saw the game, and then I go
    C. saw the game, and then I went
    D. seen the game and then I went

B. Choose the version of the underlined portion that improves the original sentence. Circle the letter of the answer you consider correct.

(21–22)   11. Sailing through the <u>inlet, his attention was caught by</u> a water skier.

    A. inlet, his attention was caught by
    B. inlet, his eye noticed
    C. inlet, he noticed
    D. inlet, his concentration was broken by

(17–19)   12. <u>In "The Monkey's Paw," it tells</u> the story of three unlucky wishes.

    A. In "The Monkey's Paw," it tells
    B. In "The Monkey's Paw" it tells
    C. The Monkey's Paw tells
    D. "The Monkey's Paw" tells

(17–19)   13.   We <u>sailed across the bay by sailboat and met up with some friends.</u>

     A.   sailed across the bay by sailboat and met up with some friends.
     B.   sailed across the bay and met some friends.
     C.   sailed across the bay and met up with some friends.
     D.   sailed across the bay by sailboat and met some friends.

(21–22)   14.   <u>Unless our camp</u> is plagued with black flies in June, I prefer to go in July.

     A.   Unless our camp
     B.   Because our camp
     C.   Although our camp
     D.   However, our camp

(21–22)   15.   <u>Despite leaving school early, numerous delays</u> caused Jennifer to miss the bus to Springfield.

     A.   Despite leaving school early, numerous delays
     B.   Though she had left school early, numerous delays
     C.   Because she had left school early, numerous delays
     D.   Though she had left school early numerous delays

C.   Each of the following sentences has an underlined error. Find the underlined section and circle the letter to identify the error.

(161)   16.   Playing Martina in singles <u>was</u> a <u>real</u> good test of Zina's <u>concentration</u>
                                    A   *B*   *C*

         in <u>critical</u> matches.
            D

         A   B   C   D

(146–148)   17.   The great artist Bruegel, <u>interpreter</u> of <u>peasant</u> life, created a
                                           A   *B*

         masterpiece showing <u>various</u> <u>childrens</u> games.
                          C   *D*

         A   B   C   D

(158–159)   18.   When I entered the auditorium, I <u>found</u> Essie <u>setting</u> in the last
                                                 A   *B*

         row, <u>practicing</u> her presentation to the <u>senior</u> class.
              C   *D*

         A   B   C   D

(35–37)   19.   If I want outdoor <u>exercise</u> <u>that</u> keeps me warm, I like <u>jogging,</u>
                                   A   *B*   *C*

         snow shoveling, and <u>to cut firewood</u>.
                           D

         A   B   C   D

(159) 20. Mr. Willis <u>learned</u> me that the shortcut was not the <u>wisest</u>
_A$$_B

<u>procedure</u> to follow in <u>solving</u> the math problem.
_C$$_D

A   B   C   D

(151–153) 21. Raul <u>throwed</u> the football far <u>down</u> the field, <u>but</u> his receiver had
_A$$_B$$_C

no way of reaching the <u>elusive</u> ball.
_D

A   B   C   D

(193–194) 22. Marge seems <u>slow</u> sometimes, but is <u>their</u> anyone quicker than
_A$$_B

<u>she</u> in going out of her way to help <u>others</u>?
_C$$_D

A   B   C   D

(156) 23. Neither Jill <u>nor</u> her brothers <u>have</u> <u>spoke</u> to their father about
_A$$_B$$_C

<u>borrowing</u> the car for the night of the dance.
_D

A   B   C   D

(192–193) 24. A <u>business</u> letter often <u>concludes</u> with the <u>complimentary</u> close
_A$$_B$$_C

"Sincerly yours,."
_D

A   B   C   D

(143) 25. My <u>father's</u> <u>cousins</u> usually spend their <u>holidays</u> in <u>countrys</u> not previ-
_A$$_B$$_C$$_D

ously visited.

A   B   C   D

D. Read all four numbered sentences. Circle the letter of the best order to arrange the sentences into a logical paragraph.

(38) 26. 1. Others recommend some form of hydrocortisone.
2. No matter what remedy is applied, the sting will hurt.
3. A sudden sharp pain announces the burning sting of a hornet.
4. Some authorities suggest applying vinegar to the sting as soon as possible.

A. 2—4—3—1
B. 3—4—1—2
C. 1—3—2—4
D. 4—1—3—2

(38)   27. 1. My great-great-grandparents used to listen to it by the hour.
             2. On closer examination, I saw it was an old gramophone.
             3. As I entered the room, I noticed a strange object at the left.
             4. This primitive machine played cylinders instead of records.

             A. 1—2—4—3
             B. 4—1—3—2
             C. 2—4—3—1
             D. 3—2—4—1

(38)   28. 1. Finally, she enjoys deceptively simple computer games like the Giant and the Dwarfs.
             2. Dot's favorite hobbies all challenge the mind.
             3. Then there's the Rubik Cube, an innocent-looking but maddening bundle of frustration.
             4. First, there's chess, an ancient trap for the unwary.

             A. 2—4—3—1
             B. 1—3—4—2
             C. 2—1—4—3
             D. 4—3—2—1

(38)   29. 1. Thus, people are willing to inconvenience themselves or even pay for having their trash recycled.
             2. This positive trend should be continued or expanded into the future.
             3. Education has brought the general public to the idea that our resources are not unlimited.
             4. Recycling has changed from a practice by the few to a general acceptance of the whole concept.

             A. 1—3—2—4
             B. 3—1—4—2
             C. 4—1—3—2
             D. 2—1—4—3

(38)   30. 1. A current dispute among scientists is the possibility of creating artificial intelligence.
             2. Though both sides maintain the correctness of their position, the argument is likely to continue for years to come.
             3. On the other side, the opponents point to certain elements that are distinctly human, unavailable to any computer.
             4. The proponents of AI, as it is called, assume that a computer will ultimately match the human mind in flexibility and resourcefulness.

             A. 1—4—3—2
             B. 1—4—2—3
             C. 2—3—4—1
             D. 4—3—2—1

E. The following paragraph lacks a topic sentence. After you have read the paragraph, follow the directions.

> Instead of stabilizing the beaches, jetties actually fight nature and eventually help destroy the beaches they were meant to protect. If we let beaches move naturally, they eventually replenish themselves. Over a long period, a shoreline is stabilized by the ceaseless ebb and flow of water and sand. But houses are built too close to beaches. Owners want to establish permanent boundaries. Jetties are supposed to provide such stability, but, to quote a marine geology professor, ''Virtually all of our coastline from New England to Texas is experiencing significant beach erosion.'' Though jetties may protect small areas, they cause disaster on beaches farther away, often threatening small towns like South Cape May in New Jersey. As long as beachfront areas continue to be developed, stopgap measures will probably be taken to save areas at the expense of the entire shoreline.

(38–39)   31. Circle the letter of the best topic sentence.

   A. A house at the seashore will always be a desirable residence as a first or second home, even though it is expensive.
   B. Some towns are being threatened by the restless movement of sand and water—for example, towns on the New Jersey coast.
   C. Jetties are the best protection against beach erosion and changing shoreline and should be built more often.
   D. Jetties built along our seashores seem like a good idea, but they actually cause considerable damage.

F. Read the following paragraph and follow the directions at the end.

> (*a*) Greedy collectors are plundering the past and destroying history in the process. (*b*) All over the world, thieves are ransacking old burial grounds, overturning monuments, stealing artifacts, and selling their booty for profit. (*c*) Though there are federal, state, and international laws prohibiting such thievery, the thefts go on because there are art dealers and collectors who don't insist on the proper sources for the objects they buy. (*d*) It is often fascinating to attend an art auction and see how collectors bid against each other. (*e*) Sometimes enforcement is difficult because juris-

diction is spread among several agencies. (*f*) In the West, for example, areas are vast, and protection suffers from too few agents, as well as shared responsibility. (*g*) Professional scavengers use off-road vehicles, skis, citizens'-band radios, and heavy equipment. (*h*) Since they do most of their work at night, they are difficult to catch. (*i*) Some authorities say that the only solution is education of both diggers and buyers to teach the value of the resources. (*j*) As hobbyists cooperating with protection agencies, the former raiders could make a contribution and have fun in the process.

(38, 40) 32. Circle the letter of the sentence that does not belong in the paragraph.

a   b   c   d   e   f   g   h   i   j

G. Circle the letter of the underlined word or punctuation mark that is incorrect. If the sentence contains no error, circle E.

33. Airplane crashes are spectacular disasters (A) rating world headlines, (B) but automobiles kill a thousand times more (C) people than do air crashes. (D) No error. (E)

34. The largest Antarctic (A) animal living (B) permanently on land is a wingless fly, it (C) is only (D) a quarter of an inch long. No error. (E)

35. "When are you planning to take (A) the Scholastic Aptitude (B) Test," (C) asked Jerry. (D) No error. (E)

36. In Europe, do womens (A) shoe sizes (B) correspond to shoe sizes in America, (C) or are (D) different numbers used? No error. (E)

37. The Victoria regia, giant among all the water lilies, (A) have (B) leaves so (C) large they can support a young child, like (D) a raft. No error. (E)

38. Tanya's car is the red convertible with sleek lines; our's is that
    $\underline{}$ $\underline{}$ $\underline{}$ $\underline{}$
    A   B   C   D
    old sedan with the faded brown finish.   No error.
                                              $\overline{}$
                                              E

39. Unlike the civilizations of China, Sumeria, and Babylon, ancient
    $\underline{}$ $\underline{}$
    A   B
    Egypt recorded the name of its greatest architect, Imhotep.
                              $\underline{}$ $\underline{}$
                              C   D
    No error.
    $\overline{}$
    E

40. Our principal spoke for the benefit of the local recycling drive, and
        $\underline{}$ $\underline{}$
        A   B
    we were agreeably suprised at the number of volunteers.
            $\underline{}$ $\underline{}$
            C   D
    No error.
    $\overline{}$
    E

41. I think the funniest essay that any American has ever wrote is James
              $\underline{}$ $\underline{}$ $\underline{}$
              A   B   C
    Thurber's "The Night the Ghost Got In."   No error.
    $\underline{}$ $\overline{}$
    D   E

42. Rushing out of doors to see the falling stars, the full moon caught
    $\underline{}$ $\underline{}$ $\underline{}$
    A   B   C D
    our attention first.   No error.
                              $\overline{}$
                              E

H. Circle the letter of the words that best complete the newly constructed sentence. Keep the meaning of the original sentence or sentences.

(21)   43. After working on the crossword puzzle for two hours, Betsy decided it was time for lunch.

Rewrite the sentence, beginning with:
Betsy decided it was time for lunch
A. but she had worked on the crossword puzzle for two hours.
B. after she had worked on the crossword puzzle for two hours.
C. being she had worked on the crossword puzzle for two hours.
D. and she had worked on the crossword puzzle for two hours.

(21)   44. In order that everyone might be served at the picnic, all the volunteers arrived early.

Rewrite the sentence, beginning with:
All the volunteers arrived early
A. although they served everyone at the picnic.
B. while serving everyone at the picnic.
C. for the major purpose of serving everyone at the picnic.
D. to serve everyone at the picnic.

(173)   45. We enjoyed swimming and water polo at the beach. We also engaged in scuba diving.

Rewrite the sentence, beginning with:
At the beach, we enjoyed swimming,
A. water polo, and scuba diving.
B. water polo and we also engaged in scuba diving.
C. and we enjoyed water polo and scuba diving.
D. and water polo. Scuba diving was also enjoyable.

(21)   46. In addition to being totally free of cancer, the Hunzas of northwest Kashmir are long-lived.

Rewrite the sentence, beginning with:
The Hunzas of northwest Kashmir are long-lived,
A. although they are totally free of cancer.
B. and cancer does not totally afflict them.
C. besides being totally free of cancer.
D. when they are totally free of cancer.

(21, 29–30) 47. Sometimes an opportunity arises. Then Caroline tries to see grand opera.

Rewrite the sentence, beginning with:
Caroline tries to see grand opera
A. whenever the opportunity arises.
B. and the opportunity sometimes arises.
C. even though the opportunity arises.
D. since the opportunity arises.

I. Read each of the following paragraphs and study the choices below it. Within the paragraph, circle the letter of the word or phrase below that best completes each sentence. Read the entire paragraph before making your choice.

(38)   48–50. The secret of good pancakes is threefold: (48) A B C D, the ingredients must be excellent. (49) A B C D, the griddle   must   be   just   the   right   temperature. (50) A B C D, the cook must know how to ladle the heavenly concoction onto the just-right surface.

A. Finally   C. On the other hand
B. First   D. Second

(67)   51–53. A first visit to the Taj Mahal is overpowering. (51) A B C D, the reflecting pool captures the radiance of this beautiful memorial. (52) A B C D the building, four   minarets   frame   the   gleaming   structure. (53) A B C D, however, is the gem itself, with its lustrous marble dome.

A. In the center   C. At the very front
B. Behind   D. Around

(38)   54–57. The story of the famous horse Snowman is inspiring.
(54) <u>A   B   C   D   E</u>, the horse was slated for death.
(55) <u>A   B   C   D   E</u>, a horse owner noticed an admirable
spirit in the doomed horse.   (56) <u>A   B   C   D   E</u>, the horse
had a special look in his eye that captured an onlooker's fancy.
(57) <u>A   B   C   D   E</u>, if it hadn't been for a perceptive buyer,
Snowman would have been destroyed.

    A. Nevertheless   D. Second
    B. However   E. Besides
    C. Originally

J. Circle the letter of the sentence that has correct sentence structure.

58. A. When plague is untreated in parts of Asia, as many as 90% of those afflicted will die.
    B. Strangely enough, antibiotics were used before the 20th century, early folk medicine called for moldy food to fight infections.
    C. The key having fallen behind the dresser.
    D. A huge oak tree dominating the forest for miles around.

59. A. Where did you leave the bottle of milk, I brought it home at noon.
    B. The Circus Maximus in Rome first held 150,000 spectators, later the number was increased to a quarter of a million.
    C. On the stage, just after the entrance of the leading man.
    D. A parrot can close its beak with a force of 350 pounds per square inch.

60. A. To survive, a bird must eat at least its own weight every two days, a growing baby bird needs much more.
    B. Because an ostrich egg is 6–8 inches long with a very thick shell, it takes about 40 minutes to hardboil.
    C. Canadian football is played on a larger field, it is characterized by a great deal of passing and high scoring.
    D. Hank Aaron, holder of a record for the greatest number of home runs in a lifetime.

K. Circle the letter of the sentence that has correct capitalization.

61. A. Carnegie Hall, a perfect concert auditorium, is still used in New York City for Symphonies and other presentations.
    B. The planet mercury is so close to the sun its surface temperature is extremely hot.
    C. Dad called out, ''where is my screwdriver?''
    D. The Southwest contains many examples of Indian ruins.

62. A. The *Reader's Digest*, a perennially popular magazine, summarizes articles in the nation's periodicals.
    B. William the conqueror defeated King Harold at the Battle of hastings, thus settling the fate of England from then on.
    C. The fairy tales of the Brothers Grimm are unfair to women, with many more evil Stepmothers than Stepfathers.
    D. Queen Victoria raised her son, the prince of Wales, strictly and unsympathetically.

63. A. At thanksgiving, we visited my grandmother in Seattle, Washington.
    B. Andrew Jackson High School was named after one of our most colorful presidents.
    C. *The Empire Strikes Back* followed *Star Wars* and became one of the Major hits of all time.
    D. The Declaration of Independence is one of our Nation's most precious documents.

L. Circle the letter of the sentence that has correct punctuation, including possessives.

64. A. Donna asked ''if I was going out for the field hockey team.''
    B. ''A long dispute,'' said Voltaire, ''means that both parties are wrong.''
    C. ''Life is too short to be small, said Benjamin Disraeli.''
    D. ''When is the meteor shower expected,'' said Terry, our amateur astronomer.

65. A. To keep your feet warm, strangely enough put on your hat, for most heat loss is through the head.
    B. Pablo's hobby bench included a hammer, a screwdriver, a pair of pliers, a jigsaw, and a monkey wrench, all scattered about.
    C. Marco Polo, famed adventurer from Italy once served as mayor of a Chinese city for three years.
    D. On our weeks' vacation, we had two days of steady rain, two days of sunshine, and three days of cold, cloudy weather.

66. A. If you have never read Tom Sawyer, you are missing a wonderful experience.
    B. Pat lives at 5140 Montiel Truck Trail, Jamul, CA, 92025.
    C. The astronauts' training is both intensive and extensive.
    D. Neil insists that if something is nobodys fault, it may be everybodys fault.

M. Circle the letter of the sentence that has correct spelling.

67. A. The hieght of many western mountains is deceptive because the surrounding valleys are also high.
    B. The character of Jane in *Jane Eyre* is both complicated and sympathetic.
    C. I have been studing the piano for four long years, but I still have difficulty with "Jingle Bells."
    D. In *Othello*, exitement rises over the loss of Desdemona's handkerchief.

68. A. Our gym is equiped with the latest parallel bars, horses, and trapezes.
    B. Ed would rather lose out on a tennis match than give up his leisurely breakfast.
    C. A person who takes everything to seriously is risking ulcers somewhere down the line.
    D. As citizens of Eastern Europe discovered, living in a free society is a priviledge to be cherished.

69. A. The committee argued for a busier and more challenging program for the coming year.
    B. If your looking for your science book, you left it over there, on top of the coffee table.
    C. Early arrivals benefitted by hearing the band warming up.
    D. The paint on the cieling was cracking badly, and Dad decided to repaint.

N. This test combines the previous three tests. Circle the letter of the sentence that has no errors of any kind.

70. A. Our local libary, the largest in the county, has a computerized card catalogue.
    B. Because of the electric light, Americans nowadays, on the average, sleep 1½ hours less each day than their great-grandparents.
    C. After the onrush of hungry campers, there wasn't hardly enough food left to feed a hungry puppy.
    D. Contrary to the ideas of some people, a perpetual motion machine would never work, it violates the laws of thermodynamics.

71. A. My fathers' car was chosen for durability, reliability, and low maintenance.
    B. Isaac Asimov says that the ages at which parents' die has little effect on the life span of the offspring.
    C. The taller of the twins has borrowed genes from the Swanson side of the family.
    D. Just between you and I, Rosalie should never have accepted a lesser role in the school play.

72. A. "I have never met anyone," said G. C. Lichtenberg, "who did not think it was an agreeable sensation to cut tinfoil with scissors."
    B. Though the loss of Alice's watch is regretable, it may teach her to be more careful in the future.
    C. A long-lasting drought broken at last by a heavy rain, from a tropical storm in the Caribbean.
    D. Julius Caesar, bothered by increasing traffic congestion banned wheeled vehicles in Rome during daylight hours.

PART IV

Writing Practice Tests

Writing Practice Test 1

DIRECTIONS

The following writing test consists of six parts divided into three sections. Each section will be covered in one writing period. Writing periods may be held on different days. The breakdown of sections into parts is as follows:

Section A: Writing Period 1

    Part I—Composition to Persuade

    Part II—Business Letter

Section B: Writing Period 2

    Part III—Composition to Explain

    Part IV—Report

Section C: Writing Period 3

    Part V—Friendly Letter

    Part VI—Summary, or Précis

As you prepare, keep in mind the following suggestions:

1. Be sure to read the directions carefully.

2. Remember to use the five steps in the writing process.

3. Try prewriting and then write a rough draft.

4. Revise the rough draft, paying careful attention to the organization of the paper, the paragraphing, and the correctness of the writing.

5. Write the final draft and proofread it.

Section A: Writing Period 1

Part I—Composition to Persuade

Directions: Write a composition in which you try to persuade the school librarian to accept the suggestion outlined below.

Situation: Although your local public library has a copier, your school library does not. You feel the introduction of such a machine would provide a much-needed convenience for students and teachers.

Your task: Write a composition of about 200 words persuading the librarian to install a copying machine in the library. Give two reasons for providing such a machine and explain each reason.

Suggestions:

1. Remember you are writing to the librarian.

2. Mention the frequent use of the copier in the public library.

3. Give the librarian two reasons why the copier should be installed.

4. Explain your reasons.

Section A: Writing Period 1

Part II—Business Letter

Directions: Write a business letter about the situation described below. Read all the information before you start to write.

Situation: You have ordered two tapes, *Songs of the Sixties*, through an advertisement on television. You carefully copied the address and noted the $8.95 charge for the tapes. You also noted the $2.50 shipping charge. You sent a money order for $11.45 ten weeks ago. Though the tapes were promised in 4 to 6 weeks, you have not yet received them.

Your task: Write a business letter concerning this situation to: Subscriber's Audio Club, 1203 Thousand Oaks Drive. Complete this address by using your own city or town, state, and ZIP code.

Suggestions:

1. Explain the problem clearly.

2. Be courteous in requesting immediate delivery of the delayed item.

3. Include all essential information.

4. Use correct business-letter form.

Section B: Writing Period 2

Part III—Composition to Explain

Directions: Write an explanation, using the suggestions below.

Situation: A friend has written to you, asking for help in completing a project.

Your task: Select one of the topics below and write a clear, concise explanation that will help him or her complete the project.

How to Cement a Sidewalk

How to Bake Bran Muffins

How to Lap-Quilt

How to Play Touch Football

How to Keep Score in Tennis

How to Tell a Good Story

How to Choose a PC Computer

How to Avoid Colds in Winter

How to Choose a Good Mystery

How to Plan a Week's Television Viewing

How to Operate a Sewing Machine

How a Drawbridge Operates

How a Helicopter Flies

How to . . . (Choose your own topic.)

Section B: Writing Period 2

Part IV—Report

Directions: Using the notes on page 218, write a report about the pleasures of stamp collecting. Be sure to read carefully and organize thoughtfully before you begin to write.

Situation: Your class is preparing a booklet on various hobbies. You have volunteered to write a report on stamp collecting. In preparation for this report, you have spoken to several enthusiastic stamp collectors and have examined several stamp magazines. These are the notes you took.

Collecting stamps not just for the wealthy

U.S. Postal Service actively promoting stamp collecting

A fortune on rare stamps, or pennies on cheap canceled stamps

Commemorative stamps honoring people and events

Increased knowledge of history, politics, world currencies, printing methods

Many advantages of stamp collecting

Promotional and instructional material in post offices

Interest stimulated by weekly magazines

Satisfactions of collecting not dependent on price

Stamp collecting a popular hobby around the world

Studying any stamp an education

Collectors brought together by clubs and exhibitions

Increased knowledge of geography, as of Kenya

In post office, colorful posters and book describing every U.S. stamp

Your task: Organize the notes and prepare a written report.

Suggestions:

1. Keep in mind the purpose: to become part of a hobby booklet.

2. Number the notes in order as a guide to the organization.

3. Write a rough draft and then the final copy.

4. Use all the information provided.

Section C: Writing Period 3

Part V—Friendly Letter

Directions: Write a friendly letter about the situation described below. Read all the information before you start to write.

Situation: You have just received a letter from a friend whom you haven't seen in several months. Your correspondent is excited about the strong possibility of getting a summer job at a county recreation center. He or she will assist the tennis teacher, help schedule tennis matches, and act as ballperson at tournaments. A lot of free time for tennis is part of the arrangement. The correspondent also includes some other news.

Your task: Reply to the letter. Imagine it has been received from one of your actual friends.

Suggestions:

1. Follow the how-to guide on page 86.

2. Comment on your friend's summer plans.

3. Tell what your plans are for the summer.

4. Briefly fill your friend in on news of your family and friends.

5. Use correct letter form.

Section C: Writing Period 3

Part VI—Summary, or Précis

Directions: Write a summary of a reading passage, using the model on pages 104–107 as a guide.

Situation: You have been presented with a reading passage, reproduced below.

Your task: In your summary, be sure to:

1. Read the passage carefully.

2. Decide upon the main idea.

3. Follow the how-to guide on page 103, eliminating all nonessentials.

4. First, jot down the notes containing the basic information.

5. Combine your notes in a rough draft to be used as the basis of the finished product.

6. Write a smoothly flowing summary containing only essential information.

The ambush bug is a tiny insect sometimes called the "Guerrilla of the Goldenrod." It has earned its name by preying upon much larger and seemingly more dangerous insects. With their stingers in place, wasps, honeybees, and yellow jackets seem safe from insect killers. They are not. They have a deadly enemy. As they flit from flower to flower, a tiny insect, the ambush bug, lies in wait. An unsuspecting honeybee may probe the goldenrod for its pollen. Its long, quick tongue flicks in and out as the bee flies from flower to flower. Then there is a lightning-quick movement. A forelimb reaches from the petals and clasps the honeybee's tongue. The bee tries frantically to escape, opening its wings and scrambling over the flower. No luck. The captor's hold is too strong. A long beak injects poison into the bee's neck, and the struggle ends.

The ambush bug looks insignificant. It is only a third of an inch long, but it has a heavy armor able to withstand the sting of otherwise deadly insects. Except for the moment of the hunt, the ambush bug lives a quiet life, lying motionless most of the time. Like many insects, its life is confined within the limits of one season. It lives only a summer. It must provide for continuation of the species, and so it lays its eggs among the leaf litter. There the eggs lie dormant through the winter until a new summer awakens them to life and another cycle of hunting.

END OF WRITING PRACTICE TEST 1

Writing Practice Test 2

DIRECTIONS

The following writing test consists of six parts divided into three sections. Each section will be covered in one writing period. Writing periods may be held on different days. The breakdown of sections into parts is as follows:

Section A: Writing Period 1

> Part I—Composition to Persuade
>
> Part II—Business Letter

Section B: Writing Period 2

> Part III—Composition to Tell a Story
>
> Part IV—Summary, or Précis

Section C: Writing Period 3

> Part V—Description
>
> Part VI—Personal Essay

As you prepare, keep in mind the following suggestions:

1. Be sure to read the directions carefully.
2. Remember to use the five steps in the writing process.
3. Try prewriting and then write a rough draft.
4. Revise the rough draft, paying careful attention to the organization of the paper, the paragraphing, and the correctness of the writing.
5. Write the final draft and proofread it.

Section A: Writing Period 1

Part I—Composition to Persuade

Directions: Write a composition in which you try to persuade the principal of your school to adopt or reject the plan outlined below.

Situation: Recently in your city an outstanding student has been named "Mayor for the Day" and has learned from the inside a little bit about how city government is run. Your friends and you have been discussing the possibility of having a "Student Leaders' Day" in your school. On this day, the school administration would be largely taken over by students, with a student principal, a student assistant, and even student teachers in your classes.

Your task: Decide whether or not such a plan is practical. Write a composition of about 200 words in which you persuade the principal to adopt or reject such a plan. Give at least two reasons in support of your viewpoint, and explain each reason.

Suggestions:

1. Remember you are trying to persuade the principal.

2. If you support the idea, emphasize the strong points. If you reject the idea, emphasize the dangers and weaknesses.

3. Provide at least two reasons.

4. Explain your reasons.

Section A: Writing Period 1

Part II—Business Letter

Directions: Write a business letter about the situation described below. Read all the information before you start to write.

Situation: You have purchased an insulated ice chest from your local sporting goods store. The advertising for the cooler featured a $2 rebate, obtainable from the manufacturer, Polar Industries. You sent the rebate coupon, along with proof of purchase. Two months have elapsed, but you have not yet received the cash rebate.

Your task: Write a business letter concerning this situation to: Polar Industries, 1520 Holton Avenue. Complete this address by using your own city or town, state, and ZIP code.

Suggestions:

1. Explain the problem clearly.

2. Be courteous in requesting the cash rebate due you.

3. Include all necessary information.

4. Use correct business-letter form.

Section B: Writing Period 2

Part III—Composition to Tell a Story

Directions: Write a narrative, using the suggestions below.

Situation: Your class is gathering together a booklet of anecdotes. These may be about famous people or people you know personally.

Your task: Think about interesting stories you have read about, heard about, or experienced. Be prepared to retell one story *in your own words*. Write the story simply and directly. If possible, save the punch line to the end. As usual, brainstorm ideas. Write a rough draft and then a final draft.

Section B: Writing Period 2

Part IV—Summary, or Précis

Directions: Write a summary of a reading passage, using the model on pages 104–107 as a guide.

Situation: You have been presented with a reading passage, reproduced below.

Your task: In your summary, be sure to:

1. Read the passage carefully.

2. Decide upon the main idea.

3. Follow the how-to guide on page 103, eliminating all nonessentials.

4. First, jot down the notes containing the basic information.

5. Combine your notes in a rough draft to be used as the basis of the finished product.

6. Write a smoothly flowing summary containing only essential information.

The rhinoceros, which we associate with Asia and Africa, was once abundant in North America. Primitive horses and camels also lived here. Then, like the rhino, they disappeared. The horse was reintroduced into North America by the Spaniards, but neither of the other two has survived in the wild here. There was even an effort to reintroduce the camel in the American desert, but the experiment didn't succeed. The fascinating history of the North American rhinoceros is written in the fossil record. In the last two decades alone, the number of North American rhinoceros fossils found has multiplied many times. The quality of the samples has vastly improved. These finds have enriched our understanding of the life of these incredible animals.

Ancient rhinos did not necessarily resemble the rhino we are familiar with today. There were sheep-sized runners and slower-moving grazers. Then, too, most extinct rhinos were hornless. There was plenty of food in a bountiful land, and the rhinos multiplied. What is now temperate North America was then a warm paradise, like tropical Mexico today—ideal for these picturesque animals. This was indeed a warm period. There were no polar icecaps. At the same time, there were even alligators and tropical plants in what is now Alaska. Then came a drastic change in climate. The earth entered a cooler period. The vegetation changed, and familiar foods disappeared. Life became harsher. The rhinos began to disappear from the North American scene. After 45 million years of successful adaptation, the rhino became extinct here, though it continued to survive elsewhere in the world. A long-running success story finally came to an end.

Section C: Writing Period 3

Part V—Description

Directions: Write a descriptive composition, using the suggestions below.

Situation: Your class is planning to assemble a booklet with the general title "My Dream Room." Each student will describe his or her ideal.

Your task: Plan to describe your dream room in detail. Suggest the appearance, the furniture, the lighting, the wall decorations, and any other items that occur to you. Try to keep a point of view that your readers can follow. Don't jump from left to right to left to center, etc. As usual, brainstorm your ideas and then write the rough and final drafts.

Section C: Writing Period 3

Part VI—Personal Essay

Directions: Write a personal essay, using the suggestions below.

Situation: Your class is putting out a class newspaper to be shared with another class in your school. All students are to prepare a special news item or feature.

Your task: You have been assigned the newspaper column "It Seems to Me." You are to write a personal essay in the style of newspaper columnists like Art Buchwald, Andy Rooney, or Irma Bombeck. Take a topic that you have an opinion about—for example, dating manners or barking dogs. As usual, brainstorm your ideas and then write the rough and final drafts.

END OF WRITING PRACTICE TEST 2

Writing Practice Test 3

DIRECTIONS

The following writing test consists of six parts divided into three sections. Each section will be covered in one writing period. Writing periods may be held on different days. The breakdown of sections into parts is as follows:

Section A: Writing Period 1

    Part I—Composition to Explain

    Part II—Business Letter

Section B: Writing Period 2

    Part III—Composition to Tell a Story

    Part IV—Summary, or Précis

Section C: Writing Period 3

    Part V—Description

    Part VI—Personal Essay

As you prepare, keep in mind the following suggestions:

1. Be sure to read the directions carefully.

2. Remember to use the five steps in the writing process.

3. Try prewriting and then write a rough draft.

4. Revise the rough draft, paying careful attention to the organization of the paper, the paragraphing, and the correctness of the writing.

5. Write the final draft and proofread it.

Section A: Writing Period 1

Part I—Composition to Explain

Directions: Write an explanation, using the suggestions below.

Situation: You have been asked to write a brief explanatory piece for your school newspaper.

Your task: Select one of the following topics and write a clear, concise explanation. In your composition, be sure to follow the guidelines on page 53.

Why a Summer Job Is a Good Idea

Why Camping Is a Good Vacation

Why a Foreign Language Should Be Taught in School

Why Football Is More Watchable than Baseball (or vice versa)

Why Sitcoms So Often Fail

Why the Networks Should Not Be Ruled by Ratings

Why a Dog (or some other pet) Is Better than a Cat (or some other pet)

Why Americans Should Change Their Eating Habits

Why Credit Cards Are Sometimes Dangerous

Why Television Commercials So Often Irritate

Why I Find *Webster's New World Dictionary* (or another dictionary) Most Helpful

Why Westerns (or some other kind of book) Are More Readable than . . .

Why . . . (Choose your own topic.)

Section A: Writing Period 1

Part II—Business Letter

Directions: Write a business letter about the situation described below. Read all the information before you start to write.

Situation: One of your favorite television series is not being renewed. You enjoy it and would like to see it retained in the fall schedule.

Your task: Write a business letter stating your views to CBN, 315 Hudson Street, New York, NY 10013. Give three reasons why you wish to see the program retained. Use correct letter form.

Section B: Writing Period 2

Part III—Composition to Tell a Story

Directions: Write a personal-reminiscence narrative, using the suggestions below.

Situation: The class will gather together a set of compositions, each with the title ''A Day in My Life'' or ''A Day to Remember.''

Your task: Think back about a day you'll never forget—perhaps a birthday, a surprise party, a trip to a dreamed-about place. Try to bring this day alive for your readers by selecting significant details and events that make the day memorable for you. As usual, brainstorm your ideas and then write a rough draft and a final draft.

Section B: Writing Period 2

Part IV—Summary, or Précis

Directions: Write a summary of a reading passage, using the model on pages 104–107 as a guide.

Situation: You have been presented with a reading passage, reproduced below.

Your task: In your summary, be sure to:

1. Read the passage carefully.

2. Decide upon the main idea.

3. Follow the how-to guide on page 103, eliminating all nonessentials.

4. First, jot down the notes containing the basic information.

5. Combine your notes in a rough draft to be used as the basis of the finished product.

6. Write a smoothly flowing summary containing only essential information.

A chain of life links all living things. A particular plant now growing in the tropical rain forest may some day provide a cure for cancer—if the plant doesn't become extinct first. Little-known plants around the world have already proved their worth, for many modern medications are derived from plants and shrubs. If these plants had been destroyed before their medical value was discovered, many persons now living would not have survived. Animals as well as plants often prove to be valuable in unexpected ways.

When a living organism is in danger of extinction because of overkill or the destruction of its habitat, it is declared an ''endangered species'' and is officially protected by the government. A success story is the Florida alligator, once hunted almost to extinction. A period of protection enabled it to come back. Such protection doesn't always come in time. The dusky seaside sparrow of the Florida Space Coast was ordered protected, but the protection came too late, and the dusky sparrow became extinct.

Environmentalists are becoming more vigilant. Most of us are familiar with such dramatic endangered species as the white rhino and the trumpeter swan, but even an inconspicuous creature can make the news if its habitat is threatened. One of the most unusual actions in recent years was taken by the state of Vermont. The cobblestone tiger beetle has been designated as the state's first officially protected insect. It is unlawful to kill the beetle or remove it from its habitat. ''Why bother?'' many people ask. In the complicated chain of life, no one knows what harmful results may come from destroying a link, any link, in that chain. In a sense, everything depends upon everything else. The fall of a sparrow can affect humanity. The bell that tolls for a seemingly insignificant species may toll for us.

Section C: Writing Period 3

Part V—Description

Directions: Write a character sketch of a person, using the suggestions below.

Situation: Your class is putting together a booklet of character sketches.

Your task: Select someone you know—a friend, a relative, an acquaintance, a leader in the community. Write a character sketch of that person. You may mention physical characteristics and personality traits. Help your readers to feel as though they know the person. As usual, brainstorm your ideas and then write the rough and final drafts.

Section C: Writing Period 3

Part VI—Personal Essay

Directions: Write a humorous personal essay, using the suggestions below.

Situation: Your class is gathering together a group of personal essays on the topic ''Advice to . . . .''

Your task: First, decide whom you are going to give advice to. Then, with tongue in cheek, write the essay that gives your suggestions. As usual, brainstorm your ideas and then write the rough and final drafts. Here are some possibilities, but do not be limited by them.

Advice to a New Dog (or cat) Owner

Advice to a New VCR Owner

Advice to a First-Time Camper

Advice to the Lovelorn

Advice to Someone Taking a Driving Test

Advice to a Museumgoer

Advice to a Couch Potato (TV watcher)

Advice to a Shopper

Advice to a Stamp (or some other) Collector

Advice to an Only Child

Advice to an Amateur Actor

Advice to a Person Attending a Masquerade

END OF WRITING PRACTICE TEST 3

Writing Practice Test 4

DIRECTIONS

The following writing test consists of six parts divided into three sections. Each section will be covered in one writing period. Writing periods may be held on different days. The breakdown of sections into parts is as follows:

Section A: Writing Period 1

  Part I—Composition to Persuade

  Part II—Friendly Letter

Section B: Writing Period 2

  Part III—Composition to Explain

  Part IV—Report

Section C: Writing Period 3

  Part V—Composition to Tell a Story

  Part VI—Description

As you prepare, keep in mind the following suggestions:

1. Be sure to read the directions carefully.

2. Remember to use the five steps in the writing process.

3. Try prewriting and then write a rough draft.

4. Revise the rough draft, paying careful attention to the organization of the paper, the paragraphing, and the correctness of the writing.

5. Write the final draft and proofread it.

Section A: Writing Period 1

Part I—Composition to Persuade

Directions: Write a portion of a letter to a friend persuading him or her to visit for overnight, a weekend, or a week.

Situation: You have a friend in another city. You haven't seen him or her for a while and would enjoy a reunion.

Your task: Write only that part of the letter that describes your plans and urges your friend to visit. Try to make the visit as appealing as possible. Think of all the good things you'll be doing. End with another expression of hope that your friend will be able to come. As usual, brainstorm your ideas and then write the rough and final drafts.

Section A: Writing Period 1

Part II—Friendly Letter

Directions: Write a friendly letter about the situation described below. Read all the information before you start to write.

Situation: Your friend has sent you a warm and welcoming letter to visit him or her during the spring break. Your parents have agreed to the visit.

Your task: Combine a letter of acceptance with a newsy letter. Tell how much you'll enjoy one or more of the activities your friend has mentioned. Perhaps inquire about mutual friends you might meet during the visit. Thank him or her for the invitation.

Suggestions:

1. Follow the how-to guide on page 86.

2. Tell your friend how pleased you are at being invited.

3. Add any news that might be of special interest to him or her.

4. Use correct letter form.

Section B: Writing Period 2

Part III—Composition to Explain

Directions: Write an explanation, using the suggestions below.

Situation: A friend has accepted your invitation to visit your new house. Your friend's parents will be driving him or her.

Your task: Write the directions to your house. Be accurate, complete, and clear. Be specific. Avoid such general statements as "About a mile or so, turn right onto a gravel road" or "I think there's an old house on the corner." Mention landmarks like the county courthouse or easily recognizable buildings like a church or an identifiable store. As usual, brainstorm your ideas and then write the rough and final drafts.

Section B: Writing Period 2

Part IV—Report

Directions: Using the notes below, write a report about the joys of gardening. Be sure to read carefully and organize thoughtfully before you begin to write.

Situation: Every student in the class is to prepare a report on a satisfying activity that might be enjoyed by all. The purpose is to open the eyes of other people to an activity that might otherwise be overlooked. In preparation for this report, you have spoken to other members of your family, all of them enthusiastic gardeners. You have asked your classmates about their own gardening experiences, if any. You have also examined several garden books and a gardening magazine. These are the notes you took.

Fresh tomatoes and green beans a special treat

Gardening one of pleasantest activities

Leaf lettuce from garden better than wilted commercial heads

Half hour in garden uncoils tense nerves

Three ingredients in successful gardening: faithful gardener, good seeds and plants, fertile soil

Failure if one ingredient is missing

Watching seeds sprout and grow almost magical

Gardening satisfies deep need in all of us

Cool of the morning is relaxation time

Many practical gains from gardening

Water and weeding essential

Cut flowers beautify homes

Corn fresh from plant sweeter than day-old corn

Many health benefits for gardener

Your task: Organize the notes and prepare a written report.

Suggestions:

1. Keep in mind the purpose: to prepare a report persuading others to try gardening.

2. Number the notes in order as a guide to the organization.

3. Write a rough draft and then the final copy.

4. Use all the information provided.

Section C: Writing Period 3

Part V—Composition to Tell a Story

Directions: Write a personal-experience narrative, using the suggestions below.

Situation: Your class is going to have a "guess who" contest. Each student will submit an unsigned narrative on the subject "A Historic First." Each narrative will be put into a "grab bag" and chosen by a class member, who will read his or her selection aloud to the class. The class members will try to guess who wrote each narrative.

Your task: Think about the title; then choose an event in your own life that was a historic first. Brainstorm ideas. Write a rough draft and then a final draft. Do not use names that will give you away as the writer. Here are some possible "firsts." You will think of others.

My First Date

My First Birthday Party

My First Day of School

My First Trip to . . .

My First Day in Driving Class

My First Dance

My First Attempt at Cooking

Section C: Writing Period 3

Part VI—Description

Directions: Write a descriptive composition, using the suggestions below.

Situation: You have received a letter from a pen pal abroad asking, "What does your town (or city) look like?"

Your task: Write only that part of your reply that describes where you live. Do not bother with letter form. When you describe your area, decide on a point of view and a basis of choice. Be selective. Choose only those details that leave an impression. Is your town or city busy, quiet, quaint, noisy, confusing, historic? Try to choose details that convey an overriding impression. As usual, brainstorm your ideas and then write the rough and final drafts.

END OF WRITING PRACTICE TEST 4

ANSWERS TO PRACTICES

Answers to Practice 1: Studying Conciseness (pages 18–19)

1. Alternative *b* is less wordy. It substitutes a phrase for a clause (*on the corner of Main Street and Maple Avenue*) and a word for a phrase (*historic*).
2. Alternative *a* is preferable. It substitutes a word for a phrase (*daytime*) and eliminates a repeated idea (*on the average*).
3. Alternative *a* is economical. It eliminates the pretentious expression *of the equine breed* and condenses a lengthy phrase and clause to a simple prepositional phrase.
4. Alternative *b* avoids repeated ideas (*cheap in price, efficient in use*).
5. Alternative *a* eliminates unnecessary adverbs (*carelessly, thoughtlessly, rapidly,* and *swiftly*). The ideas are already contained in the verbs *had lost* and *rushed*.

Answers to Practice 2: Choosing Clear Sentences (page 22)

1. Alternative *b* is correct. Alternative *a* has the dangling element *listening. Attention* cannot listen.
2. Alternative *a* is correct. It makes clear who won the award.
3. Alternative *b* is correct. In alternative *a*, the conjunction *and* doesn't suggest the idea of conflict; *but* does.
4. Alternative *b* is correct. *Regular* attendance isn't a cause of failure.
5. Alternative *b* is correct. Alternative *a* seems to suggest that the elbow disappeared.

Answers to Practice 3: Studying Subject-Not-First Sentences (pages 26–27)

1. The sentence begins with the phrase *long after his death*.
2. The sentence begins with the adverb *energetically*.
3. The sentence begins with the adverbial clause *although fish are natural inhabitants of the sea*.
4. The sentence begins with a participial phrase *checking the planet for life forms*.
5. The sentence begins with an appositive *a newcomer to politics*.

Answers to Practice 4: Identifying Appositives (page 28)

	Appositive	*Noun*
1.	football player	Byron White
2.	cleft	Copper Canyon
3.	playboys	sea otters
4.	emperor	Caligula
5.	experimenter	George Washington Carver

Answers to Practice 5: Studying Compound Subjects and Compound Predicates (page 30)

1. Alternative *b* has a compound subject *Ginnie* and *Tammy*.
2. Alternative *a* has a compound predicate *enrolled* and *expects*.
3. Alternative *b* has a compound predicate *helps* and *broadens*.
4. Alternative *a* has a compound subject *Presidents Ronald Reagan* and *George Bush*.
5. Alternative *b* has a compound predicate *thought* and *did have*.

Answers to Practice 6: Studying Complex Sentences (pages 31–32)

1. Alternative *b* is the complex sentence. The subordinate clause is *because wild plants may yet provide cures for presently incurable diseases*.
2. Alternative *a* is the complex sentence. The subordinate clause is *when Harvey arrived late at the meeting*.
3. Alternative *a* is the complex sentence. The subordinate clause is *because the Navajo language is difficult to master*.
4. Alternative *b* is the complex sentence. The subordinate clause is *although Berengaria, wife of Richard the Lion-Hearted, was queen of England*.
5. Alternative *a* is the complex sentence. The subordinate clause is *while Charlotte was weeding the vegetable patch*.

Answers to Practice 7: Identifying Verbals (pages 33–34)

1. Alternative *a* contains the gerund *gathering*.
2. Alternative *b* contains the infinitive *to be*.
3. Alternative *a* contains the participle *having studied*.
4. Alternative *b* contains the gerund *leaving*.
5. Alternative *b* contains the infinitive *to get*.

Answers to Practice 8: Studying Unified Structure (page 36)

1. Alternative *b* is unified. *Departure* and *arrival* are parallel.
2. Alternative *a* is unified. Alternative *b* introduces a nonparallel element, the independent clause *it is challenging*.
3. Alternative *a* is unified. It presents in two separate sentences two ideas that are not related closely enough to be joined in one sentence.
4. Alternative *b* is unified. It avoids the pile up of *who* and *which* clauses.
5. Alternative *b* is unified. It joins the parallel adjectives *loyal, friendly, healthy*.

Answers to Practice 1: Analyzing Explanations (pages 54–55)

1. Paragraph 1 is preferable. It is clear, interesting, and complete. It answers the question.
2. Paragraph 2 is inferior for these reasons:
   (*a*) It is poorly organized. It jumps around. It talks about ancient clocks, sundials, and then modern timekeepers.
   (*b*) It doesn't focus on the question. It mentions that the clockwise direction is related to the sundial, but it doesn't make the connection clear.
   (*c*) It introduces inappropriate elements, like the accuracy of modern clocks, that have nothing to do with clockwise motion.

Answers to Practice 2: Analyzing Directions (pages 58–59)

1. Paragraph 2 is clearer.
2. Paragraph 1 is inferior for these reasons:
    (*a*) It jumps around. It doesn't proceed straight to its destination. After leaving Melbourne Mall, it goes back to it.
    (*b*) It has much unnecessary information. For example, Babcock Street's connection with Palm Bay does not help the explanation.
    (*c*) It is too indefinite, with its "I'm not sure," "I believe," and "I forget." "Go out onto New Haven Boulevard" doesn't indicate right or left.
    (*d*) It is not smoothly written.

Answers to Practice: Comparing Anecdotes (pages 61–62)

1. The second narrative is more interesting.
2. The dialogue breaks up the flow, adds variety, speeds the story, and better suggests the personalities of the two speakers.
3. The lengthy opening sentence in the first narrative is economically cut in half in the second without loss of information. The second sentence in the first narrative is compressed into just eleven words. The lengthy third sentence is transformed into two sprightlier sentences.

Answers to Practice 1: Studying the Appeal to the Senses (pages 66–67)

1. touch	2. sound	3. smell	4. taste	5. sight
6. sight	7. touch	8. sound	9. smell	10. taste

Answers to Practice 2: Analyzing a Character Sketch (page 69)

1. Miss Murdstone is cold and hard, like metal. The feeling is negative.
2. *gloomy-looking; very heavy eyebrows, nearly meeting over her large nose; uncompromising hard black boxes; hard brass nails; hard steel purse; jail of a bag; heavy chain; shut up like a bite; metallic lady.* The word *hard* is used three times.

Answers to Practice: Analyzing an Essay (pages 70–71)

1. The first essay is more interesting. The second is rather dull.
2. *invention of the devil; health-giving sleep; blast this siren; cold floor; groping for a bed slipper; thrust aside; semiconscious state; jangling discord*
3. They break up the narration and give the clock a malicious personality of its own. They add a touch of humor.

Answers to Practice: Summarizing (pages 102–103)

All four answers deal in some way with the selection, but only one summarizes clearly, keeping the essential elements while omitting the nonessential.

(*a*) This summary completely fails to single out checkers as a deceptively hard game to master.

(*b*) This is the correct answer. This summary gives checkers its due as the central point of the passage.

(*c*) This summary doesn't even mention checkers, the central element in the passage.

(*d*) This summary adds something not in the original passage: that checkers attracts those who love puzzles.

Answers to Practice 1: Creating Simple Sentences with Compound Parts (page 123)

1. Mario and Carla play tennis.
2. The boat caught fire and finally sank.
3. We visited Washington, D.C., and toured the city.
4. Helen bought some roses and put them in a vase on the table.
5. The Tigers and the Lions play their games in our stadium.

Answers to Practice 2: Creating Compound Sentences (pages 124–125)

1. You may think of Dobermans as vicious dogs, but many of them are gentle.
2. Babies require care and attention, or they become sickly.
3. Lightning struck the tree, and the bark peeled off in layers.
4. Jim did not mow the lawn, nor did he trim the rosebushes.
5. The rain poured down, but the sun was shining.

Answers to Practice 3: Finding Subordinate Clauses (page 126)

1. (After the newscast ended,) I began my homework.

2. I won't leave (until Cindy arrives.)

3. The rain will get heavier (before it stops.)

4. (Although Martha loves ice cream,) she is going on a diet.

5. (When the snapshots are ready,) get them from the camera store.

Answers to Practice 4: Subordinate Clauses with WHO, WHICH, and THAT (page 126)

1. Georgia Bonesteel, (who teaches a course in lap quilting,) is a friend of Nancy's.

2. The Statue of Liberty is the sight (that greeted millions of new immigrants.)

3. Basketball, (which was invented by an American,) is now played around the world.

4. Itzhak Perlman is a man (who has overcome serious physical disabilities.)

5. One plant (that everyone should avoid) is poison ivy.

Answers to Practice 5: Making Fragments into Complete Sentences (pages 129–130)

Answers to this exercise will vary.

Answers to Practice 6: Correcting Sentence Fragments (pages 132–133)

1. I had never seen Joan before. OR Although I had never seen Joan before, I knew I would recognize her.
2. Charles changes his mind. OR Unless Charles changes his mind, he is going to the game.
3. The refrigerator made a loud noise. OR I don't know why the refrigerator made a loud noise.
4. We had packed a picnic lunch. OR After we had packed a picnic lunch, we decided to buy hot dogs and hamburgers.
5. The coach decides on a starting pitcher. OR Until the coach decides on a starting pitcher, the batting order will not be posted.
6. A blizzard hits the city tonight. OR If a blizzard hits the city tonight, we may not have school tomorrow.
7. You are a good friend of Nelda's. OR Since you are a good friend of Nelda's, I thought you would ask her to go with you.
8. We won the first four games. OR When we won the first four games, the number of fans increased.
9. We arrived at the concert on time. OR Since we arrived at the concert on time, we found our seats easily.
10. Storm clouds threatened. OR We sat on the patio as storm clouds threatened.

Answers to Practice 7 (pages 136–137)

There are a number of ways to eliminate each fragment. The following are not the only possibilities.

1. Our dog raced madly through the house in pursuit of our cat.
2. My brother planned to cut down a dead pine near the house.
3. Finding a four-leaf clover in the meadow near home delighted Sandra.
4. Hoping for an answer to her letter, Nan waited patiently.
5. We need an electrician to repair the short circuit in the wall socket.

Answers to Practice 8: Correcting Run-on Sentences (pages 138–139)

1. That cabinet is beautiful. It adds to the decor of the room.
2. Teresa enjoys swimming. Her brother Tom prefers boating and fishing.
3. Are you ready to leave? Do you have the tickets?
4. I dislike the laugh track on television comedies. The laughs sound so false.
5. The business of renting videotapes is booming. There are two new rental stores in town.

Answers to Practice 9 (page 140)

1. The Jets are a winning team because they have a good defense.
2. Maryanne practiced ballet for two hours since she is in a special performance.
3. I pulled the shade down because the light was shining in my eyes.
4. When George entered the supermarket, he went to the bakery section.
5. Julie was driving too fast, but she slowed down very soon.
6. As I opened the door, the phone rang.
7. Rosita got a good grade on the test because she studied very hard.
8. Mr. Carson doesn't jog every day, nor does he swim anymore.
9. Shake the bottle of medicine and take two drops in water.
10. She listened to the radio while she had earphones on.

Answers to Practice 1: Writing Plurals (page 144)

1. babies	6. halves	11. stories
2. bunches	7. misses	12. tanks
3. crashes	8. pinches	13. trays
4. puffs	9. ponies	14. keys
5. glasses	10. stones	15. waxes

Answers to Practice 2 (page 145)

1. mouthfuls	6. pianos
2. echoes	7. roofs
3. feet	8. heroes
4. textbooks	9. potatoes
5. sheep	10. teeth

Answers to Practice 3: Writing Singular Possessives (page 146)

1. animal's	7. igloo's
2. attorney-general's	8. sister's
3. brother's	9. nurse's
4. commander in chief's	10. week's
5. fox's	11. man's
6. girl's	12. year's

Answers to Practice 4: Writing Plural Possessives (pages 146–147)

1. athletes'	7. mice's
2. cities'	8. months'
3. salesmen's	9. parents'
4. four-year-olds'	10. searches'
5. geese's	11. trees'
6. houses'	12. wolves'

Answers to Practice 1: Keeping to the Same Tense (page 150)

1. I get up at 7:00 A.M. and take a quick shower.
2. Children splash in the neighborhood pool while the lifeguards supervise carefully.
3. The puppies play at Mother's feet as she knits quietly in the rocker.
4. The school bus was late, but I got an excuse note from the driver.
5. We hiked up the Mt. Greylock trail and rested on the summit.
6. I asked our football coach to put me on the team, but he said I was too late.

Answers to Practice 2: Choosing the Correct Principal Part of the Verb (pages 153–154)

1. At the fair, we *saw* a tractor-pulling contest.
2. The Coopers *brought* the hot dogs to the picnic.
3. Phyllis has *chosen* dramatics as her English elective.
4. Mr. Esposito *did* a good job in landscaping his yard.
5. You missed Vera. She has *gone* to the movies.
6. I have never *eaten* a more delicious dish than stuffed flounder.
7. Oh, I've *torn* my jacket!
8. Melanie has *drawn* a picture of our cabin in the Catskills.
9. I *have been* taking tennis lessons this summer.
10. The old maple tree in the forest has *fallen* at last.
11. Bud *came* late to the Camera Club meeting.
12. That old hat has *lain* on the desk for a week.
13. Yesterday's storm has *shaken* most of the apples from the tree.
14. Raul *swam* forty laps in the pool yesterday.
15. Have you *given* old clothes to the Dramatics Club?
16. As we entered town, the village clock *began* to strike.
17. During our move to Phoenix, three of our lamps were *broken*.
18. Paolo thought he *knew* the girl who had just entered the store, but he was wrong.
19. Has any quarterback ever *thrown* a football 70 yards?
20. The weather at the soccer game turned cold, and we were nearly *frozen* by the end of the game.
21. "Lazy Days" is the best composition Doreen has ever *written*.
22. Have you ever *ridden* on a Pasofino horse?
23. The noon whistle *blew* ten minutes late today.
24. Have you ever *spoken* before a full auditorium?
25. Sue has never *driven* a car at night.

Answers to Practice 3: Making Verbs Agree with Their Subjects (page 157)

1. The books on that shelf *are* biographies.
2. The coach, together with his players, *is* having pictures taken.
3. The elm and the chestnut *are* subject to a deadly disease.
4. Neither the president nor the other officers *were* present at the lecture.
5. A good food for dogs *contains* the right balance of vitamins and minerals.
6. Either the Denby Brothers or Wu Chen *is* my choice for first place in the competition.
7. The windows as well as the door *were* locked.
8. A woman representing local consumer organizations *speaks* tonight in the auditorium.
9. The two lamps on my father's desk *are* old but still in working order.
10. A hamburger or a frank *is* not enough for my lunch.
11. I was happy when you *were* chosen class president.
12. There *were* several garnets in that rock you found.

13. On top of the mountain *are* two huge boulders, easily seen from below.
14. Here *come* the clowns!
15. *Were* you surprised to find your watch in that old jacket?

Answers to Practice 4: Using Troublesome Verbs Correctly (page 159)

1. Wake up Dad. He has *lain* in that hammock all afternoon.
2. At my brother's graduation, our family was *sitting* in the third row of the auditorium.
3. Nobody can *teach* you anything if you resist instruction.
4. Please *take* this saw down to the workbench in the basement.
5. A species that cannot *adapt* to changing conditions is doomed to extinction.

Answers to Practice 1: Choosing the Correct Modifier (page 161)

1. You cannot do *well* if you don't have enough sleep.
2. The runaway truck careened *wildly* down the road before running into a ditch.
3. After only two lessons, Mary plays golf very *well*.
4. The river current was rushing too *swiftly* for safe swimming.
5. Our relay term ran *well*, but we still came in second.

Answers to Practice 2: Avoiding Double Negatives (page 162)

1. That haircut makes Brian look as if he hasn't *any* hair.
2. There isn't *any* more lemonade in the jug.
3. Pauline doesn't go *anywhere* without her pocket calculator.
4. The light was so dim I *could* hardly read the message.
5. Don't *ever* cross the street against the light.

Answers to Practice 3: Avoiding Some Common Errors (page 163)

1. *That* innocent-looking plant is poison ivy.
2. We searched all morning, but our beagle was *nowhere* to be found.
3. The *newest* show on television is a science-fiction special.
4. *Those* are the peaches I bought at the supermarket.

Answers to Practice 1: Using the Correct Pronouns as Subjects (page 165)

1. *We* students are late for class.
2. Maria and *she* are fond of swimming.
3. When I'm reading, nobody else can be as happy as *I*.
4. Tod and *I* went to the Lakers-Celtics game.
5. Sharon, Mike, and *he* are studying together.

Answers to Practice 2: Using the Correct Pronouns as Objects (page 166)

1. Mike bought shakes for him and *me*.
2. Joyce saw Greg and *them* on the bus.
3. The coach awarded letters to all of *us* members of the team.
4. We found our cat Max and *her* asleep in the hammock.
5. Play with Ralph and *me* in the band concert.

Answers to Practice 3: Making Pronouns Agree with Their Antecedents (page 167)

1. A girl leaving the store stumbled and dropped *her* ice-cream cone.
2. Marilyn has a new dress, but has not worn *it* yet.
3. Michael knows that *he* will make the team.
4. Janice likes cats, but Adele hates *them*.
5. The building will have *its* roof repaired.

Answers to Practice 4: Making Personal Pronouns Agree with Indefinite Pronouns (page 168)

1. Someone on the girls' field hockey team forgot *her* hockey stick.
2. No one on the swimming team gave *his or her* approval to the coach's plans.
3. An elephant forms a close bond with *its* trainer.
4. Neither Boris Spassky nor Bobby Fischer kept *his* chess title for very long.
5. Everybody brought *his or her* own golf clubs.

Answers to Practice 5: Making Verbs Agree with Indefinite Pronouns (page 169)

1. Either Paul or she *is* running in Saturday's marathon.
2. Nobody in the class *is* satisfied with the wall decorations.
3. A few of the audience *are* leaving before the end of the play.
4. One of the rear tires *has* gone flat.
5. Both of the children *were* late to school because the bus broke down.
6. Neither Kim nor his two sisters *are* above the age of twelve.

Answers to Practice 6: Choosing Correct Possessive Pronouns (page 170)

1. The idea for improving the lunchroom is *theirs*.
2. The Joneses own the Chrysler. *Ours* is the Ford.
3. *It's* starting to rain. Cover the chairs.
4. Ms. Maloney is *everybody's* favorite history teacher.
5. The book of Emily Dickinson's poems is *hers*.
6. Is this *someone's* science textbook?
7. The puppy limps because it injured *its* paw.
8. The accident was *nobody's* fault.
9. The Wilsons spent Thanksgiving with friends of *theirs*.
10. *It's* time for a new ribbon in the typewriter.

Answers to Practice 1: Writing Correct End Punctuation (page 172)

1. Where did you put the hammer?
2. Please pass the butter.
3. How beautiful that sunset is!
4. Why didn't you cut the lawn?
5. The word *paper* comes from the Egyptian word for papyrus.

Answers to Practice 2: Punctuating Correctly (pages 174–175)

1. Saturday was a dark, cold, dreary day.
2. The leopard, like the lion, is an outstanding hunter.
3. No, I strongly object to your remarks.
4. Did you ever find your missing notebook, Tammy?
5. Blue, not red, is Sue's favorite color.
6. Marilyn, however, prefers green, especially light green.
7. Vince is a fine swimmer, diver, golfer, and soccer player.
8. Are you aware that George Washington, our first President, served two terms?
9. William Henry Harrison, on the other hand, served only a month.
10. The rutabaga, or yellow turnip, is my favorite vegetable.

Answers to Practice 3: Punctuating Dates and Addresses (pages 177–178)

1. The Massachusetts Bureau of Markets is located at 100 Cambridge Street, Boston, MA 02202.
2. Was it July 16, 1969, when the *Apollo 11* lunar expedition set out for the moon?
3. The United Negro College Fund has offices at 500 East 62 Street, New York, NY 10001.
4. Write to the Lyndon B. Johnson National Historical Park, P.O. Box 329, Johnson City, TX 78636.
5. John Adams and Thomas Jefferson died on July 4, 1826, exactly fifty years after signing the Declaration of Independence.

Answers to Practice 4: Punctuating Quotations (pages 179–180)

1. "Let's go fishing in Murray Creek," suggested Alice.
2. Ron replied, "I promised Dad I'd trim the hedge."
3. "What book did you choose for a report?" asked Mr. Peterson.
4. "That was a great play!" yelled Paul.
5. "It was the first time," said Alice, "that I've thrown the ball that far."

Answers to Practice 5: Writing Titles (page 181)

1. *The Red Badge of Courage* is the book I have decided to read.
2. The newspaper *Newsday* has many readers, but not as many as the *Times*.
3. Did you see *The Color Purple*?
4. She wrote a story called "After Dark," which was published in *Seventeen* magazine.
5. "Young Love" was my mother's favorite song.

Answers to Practice 1: Capitalizing Correctly (pages 185–186)

A. 1. Dear Mr. Keane:
   2. Your friend,
   3. Dear Henry,
   4. Sincerely yours,
   5. Dear Mr. Thomas:
   6. Yours very truly,

B. 1. Once Dan Rather ended his newscast by saying, ''Courage.''
   2. ''Do you know,'' asked the teacher, ''who serves as the Secretary of State?''
   3. ''Please do your homework before you go out,'' said her mother.

C. ''Where were you born?'' asked the interviewer.
   Marian said, ''I was born in Columbus, Ohio.''
   ''When did you move to North Carolina?''
   ''In 1990, when my father accepted his new job here.''

Answers to Practice 2 (page 188)

The following words should be capitalized:

1. London
2. Republican
3. English
4. Saturn
5. Fourth, July
6. John Jay High School
7. *Raiders*, *Lost Ark*
8. Grandma, Aunt Louise
9. Southwest, Phoenix
10. Fire Island National Seashore

Answers to Practice 1: Spelling Correctly (pages 191–192)

1. excitement
2. necessary
3. committee
4. library
5. surprise
6. benefit
7. All right
8. immediately
9. character
10. certain

Answers to Practice 2 (page 193)

1. advertisement
2. appreciate
3. secretary
   writing
4. Wednesday
5. recommend
6. business
   Tuesday
   Thursday
7. delivery
8. separate
9. receive
   prompt
10. magazine
    February

Answers to Practice 3 (page 194)

1. quite
2. There
3. Where
4. lose
5. accept
6. than
7. whether
8. you're
9. too
10. It's

Answers to Practice 4 (page 195)

1. briefly
2. weigh
3. neighbor

4. height
5. ceiling

Answers to Practice 5 (page 196)

1. carefully
2. casually
3. unusually

4. cordially
5. intentionally

Answers to Practice 6 (page 196)

1. Adversity
2. whiter
3. experiencing

4. receiver
5. desirable

Answers to Practice 7 (page 197)

1. excitement
2. hopelessly
3. careful

4. Safety
5. lovely

Answers to Practice 8 (page 198)

1. hurried
2. drying
3. busier

4. supplied
5. replying
6. sprayed

Answers to Practice 9 (page 199)

1. roaming
2. swimmer
3. planning

4. stopped
5. failed

Answers to Practice 10 (page 200)

1. preferred
2. regrettable
3. benefited

4. differed
5. excelling

INDEX